WEDGWOOD

MAGNA BOOKS

WEDGWOOD

Wolf Mankowitz

THIRD EDITION

MAGNA BOOKS

© Wolf Mankowitz 1953, 1966, 1980
This edition published 1992 by
Magna Books, Magna Road, Wigston,
Leicester LE18 4ZH. Produced by the
Promotional Reprint Company Limited.

ISBN 1 85422 308 9

Printed in China

PREFACE

WEDGWOOD was, for the great collectors of the past, either blue jasper or black basaltes, and in all commentaries on Wedgwood much is written of them. But the earliest Wedgwood products, those closely related to the traditional Staffordshire pottery, have not received due attention. Either because they are rarely marked, or because they are not so different from the work of other potters, the *pineapples*, and the *cauliflowers*, the coloured glazed wares which Wedgwood developed and produced in his first five years as a master potter, have been passed over by collector and commentator alike. Yet, elsewhere the earliest examples are the most highly prized, and their origins are eagerly investigated.

Similarly, the queensware table-wares which Wedgwood developed out of the cream-coloured body he inherited from Whieldon, have been awarded less consideration than their virtue and significance deserve. For Wedgwood Queensware was the first English pottery manufactured on a large scale which for elegance, perfection of potting, and range of decorative style, could compete successfully with the porcelain productions of the Continent. Through its virtues, far more than through the qualities of his imitative Graeco-Roman styles, Wedgwood won the markets and esteem of the world. In the present work, therefore, Wedgwood's useful wares are treated as being quite as important as the more spectacular imitative bodies which he invented.

What the collector requires to know of a ceramic ware is as much technical as it is historical. To estimate the period of manufacture of a ware it is essential to know something of methods and conditions of manufacture. Marks are both helpful and misleading, for most people read rather than study them. But the qualities of a ceramic body are imparted to it by techniques of manufacture. These techniques are a part of history, and though pageants may be arranged, history can never be relived. If we learn by handling and study the specific qualities produced in a ware by the historical circumstances of its manufacture, we will not be so dependent upon marks, and as a consequence, so natural a prey to the copyist.

In order to assist the collector — for written information can only be an assistant to experience in handling — the present work concentrates on the experimental history and specific qualities of the various wares developed by the first Wedgwood, and to a much lesser extent, by his son.

It is hoped, therefore, that this book will answer some of the outstanding needs of the serious Wedgwood collector; from which category the educated dealer is by no means excluded. The dealer, after all, invests much time and money in the objects in which he deals, and as those objects become scarcer so he begins to resemble more and more in behaviour, the intent collector.

Possibly the scarcity of fine objects has contributed more to the education of both dealers and collectors than any other factor of the past twenty years. We can no longer rely on the educative effects of handling a vast bulk of goods regularly and at small risk. We must search harder, examine more carefully and invest more money than ever before.

The *serious* dealer today is a man with a *serious* interest in the objects as well as the values in which he deals; although there has never been any reason to assume that he appreciated objects less because he bought them in order to sell again. Although it constitutes no criterion, it is a notorious fact that people value most those things which cost them dearly, whether in suffering or in money. To a collector the things he collects mean very much more than their value in sterling or some harder currency. The dealer is subject to the same illogical human impulse; to attribute subjective significance to *objets d'art*.

The greatest collectors have never been mere passive accumulators, and the greatest dealers never mere merchants dispensing objects with the unconcern of cashiers exchanging one currency against another. Remembering these things we will not make the unintelligent mistake of assuming that connoisseurship is a *snobbisme* practised for the express purpose of increasing the price of inferior goods. On the contrary, it is the informed taste for particular objects alone which preserves them from the rubbish-heap and gives them value. Further, it is this informed taste which preserves the values other than monetary embodied in objects of virtue. Dealers, collectors, and objects, all need properly organized information as much as they need each other.

For many years the wares known generically as *Wedgwood* caused little interest in the auction-rooms or the antique shops when they appeared. When the Barlow Collection of Old Wedgwood was sold at Christie's in the 'eighties, a fine jasper bas-relief of Paccetti's *Sacrifice of Iphigenia* brought 120 guineas. In 1945, a good year for the antique trade, the same bas-relief could be bought for £20, and it was not easy to find buyers. The fact of the matter was that the principal collectors of Wedgwood flourished in the years preceding the 1914 War. Barlow, Sibson, Tangye, Falcke, Rathbone, are all names in Wedgwood collecting tinged with the nostalgic hue of the secure world which enjoyed an indian summer in the few years following the death of Queen Victoria. The reaction against Victorianism which followed the first World War, tossed Wedgwood into the limbo of Victorian taste, and left it forgotten there. Because the tycoons of the last century competed fiercely for its possession, old Wedgwood wares commanded high prices. Because those imperative old gentlemen were dead and their tastes and achievements sneered at by the inheritors of their imperialism, prices sank and the wares were left desolately in the attic.

The public's association of Wedgwood's classic eighteenth-century perfection with Victorianism, was certainly irrational. Nevertheless it was complete. In Wedgwood the 'modernist' could find the restraint and scrupulous balance, the concern for stability, the high valuation of industry, qualities decorative and decorous against which the post-war world militated. Feelings which appeared to be new because of their violent manifestation demanded forms apparently new enough to accommodate them. Antiques were by and large left to the itinerant American to collect and carry home. Europe was more interested in objects expressing the fluid experience of naive craftsmen in primitive societies refreshingly un-European. The nineteenth century, it was felt, was conspicuous for its repression of dynamic movements and its sheer lack of taste. The eighteenth century, with its narrow insistence on 'Reason' and its self-consciously classical urbanity, might occasionally be amusing or elegant, but was sadly out of key with that contemporary discovery, 'the modern world'. In consequence, the antique trade in the 'twenties once and for all orientated itself upon the fact of the apparently inexhaustible American collector — a buyer both shrewd and hysterical, indiscriminately acquisitive, but fast becoming the most faithful and exacting of all clients.

Though the American market may well be inexhaustible, goods to supply it cannot in all cases be ordered from factories eager and able to sell as much merchandise as they are asked for. The trade in deliberate or silent fakes has been and is considerable, but it has never been greatly important. No buyer who is or who will become a collector in the serious sense buys more than a very few fakes, and those only at the stage when collecting is fresh upon him and the down on his knowledge has not yet been rubbed off by an expensive mistake or two. What fakes or imitations are sold are largely supplied to buyers who wish to give a cultivated impression to friends with as little knowledge or flair as themselves. As every dealer knows, such people, no matter how extravagant they may be in their selection of cars, furs, holiday resorts, and the other more conspicuous displays of wealth, are normally unable to perceive the difference between Wedgwood jasper and cheap blue bisque from some French factory. Such buyers have rigid notions of objective value. They may occasionally be tripped by a deft salesman into purchasing an authentic piece, but it is almost certain that the first low-priced copy they see will make them regret their imprudent connoisseurship. It is to this market that the fake is addressed. It is a market profitable enough to those who supply it, but of no value at all to the serious antique trade. Its eagerness for the bargain with apparent virtue wraps all objects in miasmal confusion resolved only by price tickets marked in plain figures.

But the important buying public in America is not of this uneducated and largely uneducable class. A vast market will always exist there for cheaper and inferior goods with pretensions, but its buyers are mere apes of fashion. They can never become collectors, while the dealers who supply them remain traders who would be just as satisfied to sell tinned meat, practical jokes, or patent medicines.

Beyond the comprehension of both traders and buyers at this elementary level, is the expanding society of collectors with serious and informed interest in objects, and an urgent sense of their importance. These collectors and the dealers who supply them know that without informed taste the objects with which they are concerned will lose every kind of value. To them this book is addressed.

There are some who enjoy the prospect of a dealer-less and collector-less society; but intelligent professional artists and craftsmen know they could not persist for long without engaging the interest of the dealer and his client. The truth is that if objects of no assessable objective worth are to be exchanged against money, then there must be both those who are able to arrange the exchange and those whose taste and knowledge enables them to determine appropriate values. In this activity connoisseurship is a code of the genuine, the warranted, the carefully and thoroughly attested. It is to the revived connoisseurship of Wedgwood that this book is dedicated.

30th March, 1953   WOLF MANKOWITZ

Publisher's Note on the Third Edition

This new edition is produced to coincide with, and celebrate, the 250th anniversary of the birth of Josiah Wedgwood I. It is therefore available again for ceramic historians and all collectors of Wedgwood, now with some necessary minor changes and new information.

1980

CONTENTS

ACKNOWLEDGMENT

GRATEFUL thanks are due to Messrs. Josiah Wedgwood & Sons for making records, information and other material available; to Mr. Tom Lyth, Curator of the Wedgwood Museum; to Mr. Morley Hewitt; to Colonel M. H. Grant; to Mr. Geoffrey Bemrose; to Sir Ralph Wedgwood, Bt.; to Mr. John H. Wedgwood; to Mr. Hensleigh Wedgwood; to Mrs. Ann Finer; and to my secretary, Miss Patricia Paterson, for the immense assistance they have given me. I should like to acknowledge too the invaluable work of the Wedgwood Club of America and its members, who for the past twenty years have researched with understanding and great diligence into the subject; their published papers have been of the highest value to the study of English ceramics.

All the illustrations are reproduced by kind permission of Messrs. Gered, Messrs. Josiah Wedgwood and Sons, and private sources acknowledged in the text.

WOLF MANKOWITZ
1953

LIST OF ILLUSTRATIONS

COLOUR PLATES

MONOCHROME ILLUSTRATIONS

xvii

COLOURED
GLAZED WARES
1754-1764

COLOURED GLAZED WARES
1754-1764

The Whieldon-Wedgwood Partnership, Fenton Hall, 1754-9
The Ivy House Works Period, Burslem, 1759-64

IN 1739, the year in which Thomas Wedgwood, elder brother of Josiah, inherited the Churchyard Works in Burslem, the practice in the Staffordshire potteries was for 'a good workman who could *throw*, *turn* and *stouk*' to serve two or three different manufactories. The staple product of the district was the white stone-ware introduced by Astbury, and in addition to the services of a good workman who understood the basic techniques of its manufacture, a pottery required 'the slip-maker, thrower, two turners, handler (*stouker*), fireman, warehouseman, and a few children'. The practice of these crafts was poorly rewarded. John Fletcher, a workman at the Churchyard, was paid fourpence a week in his first year of employment, sixpence in the second, and ninepence for the third.[1] His work was to prepare the clay into balls for Josiah and Richard, his master's sons, both of whom were throwers, Josiah being only eleven. 'Richard', Shaw observes, 'enlisted for a soldier', a pointed enough comment on the attractions of pottery manufacture at that time.

Josiah Wedgwood, a thrower at eleven years of age, was born in July 1730 in a 'tenement' near his father's works in Burslem. There was no Free School in Burslem until 1750, and beyond being taught the elements at a local private school Josiah had little education, but in potting he was already an experienced and useful hand when, in November 1744, he was bound apprentice to his brother for a term of five years. No doubt his pattern of employment during this period was the same as that of any other 'good workman'. He worked as convenience directed at all the tasks involved in pottery manufacture, and though he never ceased to condemn the slipshod methods of potteries like the Churchyard, he owed his own excellent grounding in the industry to them. In view of his later development it is not surprising that at the age of nineteen Josiah should have considered himself fitted to enter a partnership with Thomas; it is

---

[1] According to SIMEON SHAW, *History of the Staffordshire Potteries* (1829)

equally understandable that Thomas should not have been eager to saddle himself with a talented and energetic younger partner who already entertained 'fancies' about the potteries in general and the family works in particular.

Josiah left the Churchyard in 1752 and went, it is said, to live at Stoke with Daniel Mayer, a wealthy and respectable tailor. It was in Stoke that he entered his first partnership agreement. He was, with the financial backing of a local tradesman named John Harrison, to undertake the manufacture of pottery at the factory of John Aldersea or Alders at Cliffe Bank. It is likely that his association with Alders was limited to that of a sub-tenant with the use of the factory amenities; at all events his arrangements here were terminated in 1754. By one account he was forced to leave the Cliffe Bank because of a leg, troublesome since an early attack of small-pox.[1] By another, Harrison, whose father was a banker, was unconcerned with Wedgwood's ambitions. He wanted to restrict manufacture to agate and marble knife hafts, and the cloudy, tortoiseshell, and black wares with lead or salt glazes which were common to the Staffordshire potters. These staple products offered a quick and assured return, and Harrison, remembering perhaps his father's banking principles, saw no commercial point in financing experiments on which the profits were speculative.

It is impossible to determine exactly the work Wedgwood did whilst at the Cliffe Bank. Certainly the business was not terminated for lack of trade. The most likely explanation is that Harrison feared losses resulting from Wedgwood's experimental interests, while Wedgwood himself discovered that working with another man's money made him little more than talented labour hired at slightly more favourable terms. What he must certainly have learnt from his two years with Harrison was that a potter needed to be a business man as well as a craftsman, and that if he was to instrument his manufacturing plans he required considerably more capital than the very small inheritances left to him. If he discovered this much it was perhaps enough, for it was Wedgwood's ability in later years to combine the qualities of merchant and craftsman which made him the greatest of the Staffordshire potters.

About the year 1740, Thomas Whieldon had opened a small pot-works at Fenton Low. There he manufactured mottled and marbled wares, black Egyptian, tortoiseshell plates and tea-ware. Whieldon's work, exemplifying the finest Staffordshire pottery of the mid-eighteenth century, has lent his name to the products of a whole group of potters, not all of the same excellence. Whieldon-ware itself is a fine earthenware of cream colour with glazes mottled and stained with black, grey, brown, blue, yellow, and green. In addition to this so-called 'tortoiseshell'[2] ware, Whieldon also made Elers-style unglazed red teapots, glazed red and white Astbury-style ware, solid agate, black ware of the so-called Jackfield type, and grey and white salt-glazed stoneware. The turnout of the Whieldon factory itself was very considerable and

---

[1] In the epidemic of 1747.

[2] The popularity of tortoiseshell and later styles is indicated by advertisements in the *Boston Gazette* in the years 1754 to 1770 offering 'new fashioned Turtle-shell tereens', 'Tortoise Shell Teapots' and other coloured glazed wares of the Whieldon-Wedgwood type.

when Thomas Whieldon retired in 1780 he did so with a fortune of £10,000.[1]

Although the production of his factory was large and, consequently, uneven in quality, Whieldon was a highly talented craftsman and attracted to Fenton some of the most promising of the younger potters. Aaron Wood, the modeller, Josiah Spode, and William Greatbatch, were Whieldon's apprentices, while Wedgwood, when he left Alders and Harrison in 1754, entered into a five-year partnership with him.

At this time Wedgwood was twenty-four, and Whieldon already the most important potter in Staffordshire. By their quality and attractiveness of design and glaze, Whieldon's products had gained a large enough market for his factory to expand well beyond the common limitations of his time. When Wedgwood joined him he had already carried the industry to a higher level of production and technique than would have seemed possible twenty years before. His acceptance of Wedgwood as a partner must have been conditioned by his recognition of the young man's organizational and business capacities as much as by his qualities as a potter. Whieldon, indeed, was interested in the innovations Wedgwood had in mind. He realized that the movement forwards towards greater industrialization was an inevitable one. Furthermore, the market for standard Whieldon products had been losing ground steadily and the Fenton Vivian factory needed the improvements which Wedgwood could introduce. The remarks which Wedgwood wrote in his 1759 Experiment Book describe the state of the trade succinctly, and explain the function he fulfilled in the partnership with Whieldon:

> 'This suite of experiments was begun at Fenton Hall, in the parish of Stoke-upon-Trent, about the beginning of the year 1759, in my partnership with Mr. Whieldon, for the improvement of our manufacture of earthenware, which at that time stood in great need of it — the demand for our goods decreasing daily, and the trade being universally complained of as being bad and in a declining condition.
>
> White stoneware (viz. with salt glaze) was the principal article of our manufacture; but this had been made a long time, and the prices were now reduced so low that the potters could not afford to bestow much expense upon it, or make it so good in any respect as the ware would otherwise admit of; and with regard to elegance of form, that was an object very little attended to.
>
> The article next in consequence to stoneware was an imitation of tortoise-shell, but as no improvement had been made in this branch for several years, the consumer had grown nearly tired of it; and though the price had been lowered from time to time in order to increase the sale, the expedient did not answer, and something new was wanted to give a little spirit to the business.

[1] He built a large house near Stoke, and 'was so greatly esteemed for his charity and his good works,' that he was made Sheriff of the county of Stafford in 1786. He died in 1798, having outlived Josiah Wedgwood by two years. On retiring in 1780 Whieldon dispersed his moulds. In 1829, according to Simeon Shaw, 'Whieldon's house was a deserted ruin and the factory at Fenton Low converted into dwelling houses.' The 'large house near Stoke', known as Fenton Hall became the residence of William Adams in 1818, and was demolished in 1847 to make way for a railway.

I had already made an imitation of Agate which was esteemed beautiful, and made a considerable improvement, but people were surfeited with wares of these various colours. These considerations induced me to try for some more solid improvement, as well in the body as the glazes, the colours, and the forms of the articles of our manufacture. I saw the field was spacious, and the soil so good as to promise ample recompense to any one who should labour diligently in its cultivation.'

These comments suggest Whieldon's agreement to developments which, within a very few years, were to become competely identified with Wedgwood. Because of his prodigious success and the highly individual nature of the wares he eventually developed, Wedgwood is too often presented as a potter in the margin of the native tradition. Enthusiasts for the earlier Staffordshire wares frequently give the impression that the Staffordshire potters ended with Wedgwood. Some go so far as to suggest that Wedgwood ended them by introducing production techniques and business methods with which they could not compete. In fact, of course, the industrialization of Staffordshire was an inevitable development foreseen by Whieldon, and forwarded by his activities. A growing market for pottery wares demanded of the Staffordshire potters new methods of production, while the taste of the urban buyers required new designs and eventually new wares more in keeping with their criteria of sophistication. Wedgwood, very sensibly, recognized these facts, approximating his production to a public demand which both as a craftsman and a business man he applauded.

Wedgwood's partnership with Whieldon was friendly and highly productive. Whieldon was an intelligent employer and partner. He was shrewd enough to guard his trade secrets carefully, even going to the extent of burying shards to prevent them being imitated by competitors. He had excellent trade connections, especially with the Birmingham metal mounters and silversmiths, whom he supplied with considerable quantities of snuff- and other boxes, buttons, and vanity items which when mounted found a popular market.

His own summary, already quoted, of the work Wedgwood did whilst in partnership with Whieldon is of great value in determining wares which may be certainly ascribed to the period of their association. The marked improvement of Whieldon's solid agate, and the improvement and extension of the colours in his tortoise-shell, are directly attributable to Wedgwood. In ascribing wares of the partnership years 1754–9 high quality, improved colour, shape, and modelling are safe criteria, and some of the finest work of the Whieldon factory belongs to the partnership.[1]

The 'suite of experiments' begun in 1759, the last year of the partnership, as a result of Wedgwood's experience of the market, was directed towards the invention of new wares which could be put into production when Wedgwood started on his

[1] The MS. of the partnership agreement has been lost but we know from quotations and frequent references that Wedgwood's contribution was to have been 'secrets' which he alone possessed. This, considering the fact that Whieldon's business was an important one, can only mean that in 1754 Whieldon needed new wares more than extra capital.

own account. Whieldon did not apparently object to Wedgwood's use of Fenton Hall for experimental purposes, although he must have known that the younger man would start business on his own account very soon. Wedgwood at this time would have been short of kiln space and other amenities, and may have made suitable arrangements with his former partner. Whieldon's attitude could well have been that the established business was already more than sufficient for his purposes. We do, in fact, know that after 1759 Whieldon continued to produce the wares which characterized the partnership period. Indeed so little change came about at Fenton Vivian after Wedgwood left that one commentator incorrectly states that Whieldon retired in that year.

Certainly, it was with his partner's agreement that Wedgwood undertock to engage his cousin Thomas as a journeyman. The document is preserved and is of great importance:

'Decr 30th 1758 — Memorand^m of an Agreement between Josiah Wedgwood of the Parish of Stoke in the County of Stafford, Potter, and Thos Wedgwood Journeyman now liveing at the City of Worster potter, the s^d Thos Wedgwood engageth to serve the s^d Josiah Wedgwood as a Journeyman from the first of May 1759 to the 11 of Novemb^r 1765 and is to receive of the s^d Josiah Wedgwood twenty two Pounds of lawfull money for every years service'.

This document suggests that Wedgwood planned with Whieldon's approval (since he was still with him when it was drawn up) to start business on his own account as soon as the partnership period came to an end, probably in May 1759. An experiment, bearing the date 28th March 1760 at Fenton, further suggests that Wedgwood did not entirely break his connection with Whieldon at the termination of the partnership; for if he had, the cautious Whieldon would hardly have permitted him continued use of Fenton Hall.

Wedgwood's most important discovery at this period is listed on the first page of the Experiment Book as the seventh trial in the new suite. The numbers above the line indicate materials, those below, the quantities, used. The experiment is dated 23rd March 1759.

$$7. \quad \frac{3 \qquad 17 \qquad 33}{120 \quad\; 30 \quad\;\; 9}$$ A Green glaze, to be laid on Common white (or cream color) biscuit ware. Very good.

Of this green glaze,[1] Wedgwood wrote: 'This is the result of many experiments which I made in order to introduce a new species of coloured ware to be fired along with the tortoise-shell or agate ware in our common gloss ovens, to be of an even self colour, and laid upon the ware in the form of a coloured glaze.'

Since we know that Wedgwood arranged to employ his cousin from May of that year, it is possible that he may have left Whieldon some rights in this new and

[1] Guy Green of Sadler & Green has an entry in his receipt book as follows: 'Mr. Wedgwood's Green: Flint glass 6, Red lead 2, White enamel 4, vitrified Calcin'd copper 1/12. This will be a blue green and will require a good deal of yellow.'

revolutionary green glaze. But Whieldon is unlikely to have used it to any greater extent than green had already been used in the Whieldon-Wedgwood tortoise-shells.[1] New coloured glazes were one of Wedgwood's specific experimental interests, and the satisfied Whieldon is unlikely to have bothered with them very much — especially in view of his friendly relations with the younger man. We may conclude, therefore, that the green-glazed ware was among Wedgwood's first productions after starting on his own account, and that it was first produced by him on a serious scale in 1760 at the Ivy House Works. Leaf-shaped 'useful' items were the obvious application of the solid green glaze, but it was also used on teapots, dishes and plates in patterns often attributed to Whieldon. It was immediately popular and has, since the Ivy House period, been several times revived, though without comparable quality.

Wedgwood's use of the green glaze at this time is of special importance in respect of the wares known as cauliflower and pineapple.[2] Without the fine solid green which Wedgwood developed in the last months of the partnership, these wares could not have been made. As it is, we can be sure that the first productions of the Ivy House Works at Burslem featured not only plain green-glazed items, but the cauliflower, pineapple and similar fruit wares as well, their shapes being noted in the Pattern Book for that period.

The discovery of an equally essential yellow glaze is recorded 10th March 1760 as experiment 93: 'A Tryal for yellow glaze,' and experiment No. 100, probably in April of that year records: 'Tryal for a *full yellow* Glaze.' Apparently the brilliant yellow glaze was not perfected until Wedgwood was already advanced into the Ivy House period, and it becomes more and more certain that the 'fruit' wares were Wedgwood's specific invention. Salt-glaze block moulds of both cauliflower and pineapple style pieces were, in fact, found at Etruria in 1905. But although these wares are certainly *Wedgwood*, their production is a more confused question.[3]

[1] It is significant that no solid green glaze fragments have been found in the course of excavation on the Fenton Low site.

[2] In a note in *Old Wedgwood* 1940, Mrs. Gorely points out the extraordinary excitement which the cultivated pineapple created on its introduction in the mid-eighteenth century.

[3] According to Miss Meteyard, in his last year with Whieldon Wedgwood was seriously troubled by his leg (which was eventually amputated in 1768). As a result of absence due to this disability Wedgwood was forced to entrust certain glaze experiments to workmen at Fenton, who subsequently gave the information to other manufacturers. Miss Meteyard states that Dr. Thomas Wedgwood, a distant relation who had a factory called the Ruffleys, made cauliflower ware. It seems likely too that Thomas Wedgwood (Josiah's brother at the Churchyard) also made the ware. It is possible, of course, for Miss Meteyard is violently pro-Wedgwood, that as with creamware (on which many potters were experimenting at the same time as Wedgwood) the green glaze was being simultaneously investigated by Wedgwood's more astute contemporaries. This is suggested by a letter from London dated 17th August 1763 from Thomas Wedgwood, the cousin in Wedgwood's employ who reports: 'Mr. Williams has wrote to you by today post concerning some abatment in the 12 Collyflower Tpots sent as they are too small. I see some 18ᶜ in London allmost as large as our 12ᶜ. . . .'

Who these competitors were it is not possible to state with certainty. Jealousy amongst the Staffordshire potters and their preparedness to 'steal' one another's 'secrets' would anyhow quickly bring about the general adoption of successful improvements, no matter how closely guarded.

Wedgwood's challenge to the declining Staffordshire market at this time was the novelty, green and yellow glazed ware. With it he was to lay the foundation of more ambitious developments, but his means of production were seriously restricted, and he needed at this time in his life extra facilities more than new ideas. An associate of Fenton Vivian days, William Greatbatch, was an eager party to arrangements for increasing the Ivy House turnout. A letter from Greatbatch to Wedgwood dated 31st January 1762 describes a quite specific arrangement:

'Sir

Having considered what you and I were talking about am come to a resolution to proceed and have hired men, taken a place part of which ready the rest by promise to be built by May, which when finished will begin immediately, and am preparing things in readiness. I intend to come over to Burslem as soon as opportunity offers. In the interim should be glad to have your proposals what you can afford to give per dozen for round teapots all sizes together likewise oval &c. &c. Should be glad to have an answer back the next week end by the bearer. So remain with great respect Yr. Most Oblg'd Hble. Svt.'

Wedgwood's association with Greatbatch began as far back as 1760, the first year at the Ivy House. Greatbatch's 'place' was the Lane Delph Fenton Factory. Simeon Shaw's account of Greatbatch's career is worth quoting in full. The period referred to is 1765–70.

'Another excellent modeller, and in fact a general workman of first rate abilities, was Mr. William Greatbatch, some time employed by Messrs. Whieldon and Wedgwood; and who had commenced business on his own account at the manufactory at Fenton, now small part of the extensive establishment of Messrs. Bourne, Baker and Bourne; where he produced numerous articles, of improved patterns and kinds; and for some time had a most rapid sale of teapots, on which was printed, in black, by Thomas Radford, the history of the Prodigal Son. But heavy losses at length ruined him. His well known abilities caused him to be consulted, and to form the plan, for the New Field Manufactory, then being erected by Admiral Child; from whom he was to have received a third share of the profits for managing the establishment. Mr. Wedgwood, aware of the talents of his former servant, engaged him, *for life*, at the very high wages of *five shillings* a day, whether at work or play, and house rent free; which sum was regularly paid him, to the time of his death, tho' he survived his master; by whom he was so much respected, that most of his sons, and many of his relations, were employed at Etruria.'

Greatbatch supplied Wedgwood with coloured glaze and Chinese style wares and his association with the Ivy House and the later factories became closer as Wedgwood's business developed.[1] In May 1764 Greatbatch writes as follows:

[1] Counting-house documents in the Wedgwood archives in Greatbatch's hand dated 1788 to 1807 make it clear that he was in later years employed in an executive capacity.

'There are now ready two of the Crates of the Pine Apple ware, and a large quantity of Plates — about a gross & 1-2 of Light Couler teapots & a good quantity of China tpts the same as Mr. Whieldon & other sorts.

The order of the Pine Apple ware wch Thomas (Wedgwood) gave me will be compleated the next ovenfull — his order Consist of about 80 Doz should be glad to know what sorts to make to Compleat the Order you gave — we got no cover moulds for 18 milks.

Should be glad to have your advice in the shape of the Squirrel & Bird tpt Block, & whether you would have a ground work upon it or not, the work will be Compleated to Day or to Morrow to lay on — There is one size ready of the fruit dish and stand & will make a few for your approbation . . . '[1]

Greatbatch had great respect for Wedgwood and was immensely valuable to him in Ivy House days. He seems to have organized his business as Wedgwood directed and was to all intents and purposes in the employ of the greater potter, so that the variety of wares he produced are virtually *Wedgwood*. In a postscript to a letter dated 11th November 1764, he writes:

'Have rec'd yours dated Nov 2nd & shall contract my business in a nearer compass by parting with two men this day. As to reserve in Modeling it is far from me. It is the want of a proper design which makes me neglect finishing as I would do, have sent you two unwrought draughts inclosed to have your sentiments on, was I to make them I should not follow them exactly but these by way hint to something in this way. Should be glad you should form something you think is likely to take as you understand what will suit trade better than me. If you leave it to me will exert myself the best in making a tpt first before I proceed any farther for your approbation. — It is far from me to having any thoughts of dropping our connection as long as can carry it on with any tolerable degree of advantage but I know there is an absolute necessity to have something new and shall employ the small genius I have in inventing something I hope that will be of advantage to both, so remain yours as above.'

Greatbatch associated himself humbly with Wedgwood in the effort to devise new wares, the 'absolute necessity to have something new.' He was a potter of considerable talent, and his contribution to the Ivy House was more important than former commentators have suggested. That Greatbatch grew less humble after the death of

[1] A bill from Greatbatch indicates the range of ware which Wedgwood was 'jobbing' out to him at this time for Modelling:

1 Leaf Candlestick	£0 -	4 - 0
1 Oval fruit basket & stand		12 - 0
1 Pr Conu Copia		12 - 0
3 oblong fruit dishes	£3 -	3 - 0
1 pine apple teapot		8 - 0
1 Chinese Teapot		10 - 6

Similarly the following note from Greatbatch: 'Have sent by bearer a Rec't for y^r bill sent herein inclosed — with two Crates of ware No. 140 - 9 Doz Tpts . . . 5 Cauliflower Turenes & stands. No. 141 3 Doz Tpts 12 - 8 Doz Ditto 24. . . .'

Wedgwood is indicated by a letter from Thomas Byerley to Josiah Wedgwood II:

'William G. came to Etruria in 1788 — when Thomas Wedgwood declared his intention of settling at Hill House with his family — W.G. and all his family were at the time in Turner's employ — who, on the old man going away sent all the rest after him — and they all came to Etruria — W.G. was an app. at Fenton during my late uncle's partnership there, and when he first set up at Lower Lane for some years he made biscuit ware only — for the new work at Burslem where it was sent to be coloured and glazed.

I never heard that any engagement or promise was made him to continue the whole or part of his salary during life — indeed at one time he would have quitted unless his wages had been raised £25 p. ann. — which went under the name of extra $\frac{1}{2}$ [illegible] in order to conceal that such high wages were given to anyone. This was when W. Bent had been tampering with him, and offered him higher wages, I think that he should certainly be made easy and comfortable in his circumstances for the remainder of his days — but that it is not necessary to make his present salary the basis — I think it should be [illegible] to a sum that he and his wife can live comfortably upon in their condition of life, and I think too what they possess of their own should not entirely be left out of consideration in fixing the annual sum to give him — they have two or three houses at Lane Delf what else I know not — the late W: Wood had been his entire life with you from his first working day to the day of his death — but in W.G.'s case there is not a great deal to distinguish it from that of many in the potteries, who cannot indulge expectations of this kind. W.G. has many hangers on who will urge him to scramble for all he can get — but as it is possible that principles and precedents now established, may, in the course of your life, be often quoted it is proper to proceed with caution and whatever is granted not to do it too lightly as a matter of course — I suppose all good and sound reasoning would be on the side of saving our money on such occasions, but I am not inclined to deny my feelings the gratification of a share in these discussions. . . . '

It seems that Greatbatch became a sort of ghost of the first Josiah's early days of struggle, and that after Wedgwood's death he was a cause of embarrassment to the firm's directors. The importance of the Byerley letter however, from our point of view, is that it establishes the precise function Greatbatch served in relation to the Ivy House coloured glaze wares. He was responsible for the potting and modelling, but the secret of the glazing Wedgwood kept safely in his own hands. This arrangement accounts for the variations in spouts, handles, and other details commonly found in cauliflower and pineapple wares. Such details Wedgwood left to convenience and to Greatbatch. Because of this virtual partnership, wares in these styles are hardly ever found marked with the impress which Wedgwood had already at this time generally adopted. The unmarked fruit ware should, in accuracy and fairness, be described as 'Wedgwood-Greatbatch.'

Along with solid green-glazed wares in leaf styles and the new fruit wares,[1] Wedgwood also produced Whieldon-style tortoise-shell, using the yellow and green glazes he had developed to brighten and increase their appeal. Coloured glaze items of this type are difficult to distinguish from Whieldon-ware and they are normally unmarked. But the teapoy reproduced on Plate III is impress-marked, and is consequently of the greatest importance, for it establishes beyond doubt Wedgwood's production of Whieldon-type wares at the Ivy House. The teapoy is a First Pattern-Book shape and is also found in creamware of the early period. Items in this style are distinguishable by shape[2] and type of body, which is nearer to fine Queensware than to the coarser Whieldon cream body.

Wedgwood operated the Ivy House Works until 1764. The five years of this period find him working as manager, designer, warehouse-clerk, and general overseer of every stage in the production of pottery, his small capital making close personal supervision essential as an economy, quite apart from its desirability from the point of view of the quality of his products. The careless methods which characterized workmen in the industry at this time made personnel a principal concern, and the sheer business of making pottery manufacture pay makes the Ivy House period a time of hard, systematic work to increase turnout. Aware as he was of the possibilities of new bodies, and already deeply interested in developing creamware, Wedgwood had no alternative but to give production prior consideration.[3]

Wedgwood's market at this time was the same as Whieldon's, and his wares inevitably similar to those of his former partner. But the Whieldon-style wares of the Ivy House were distinguished by their purer colour, especially greens and yellows, as well as by the new shapes which Wedgwood introduced. At the Ivy House, too, Wedgwood continued the production of the fine solid agate which he had brought to perfection while with Whieldon. Similarly, the Elers-style and Astbury-style wares still found a certain market and were consequently relevant to Wedgwood's programme of high production. Some of the redwares marked with a Chinese style seal are attributed to Wedgwood largely, it seems, because a 'W' is sometimes found incorporated in the cypher. But it is unlikely that Wedgwood would have been concerned to put his mark (and an obscure one at that) upon wares which were purely of a bread-and-butter character, or, as with redwares, likely to have been jobbed-out production.[4]

---

[1] Apart from pineapple and cauliflower wares in which teapots were the most common item, wares in the form of melons, lemons, quinces and cucumbers are referred to in contemporary orders. These latter styles are of extreme rarity. Complete sets in cauliflower and melon comprising coffee cups, saucers, chocolate cups, dishes, plates, tureens, ewers, basins and sauceboats are also mentioned. The melon style was sometimes glazed in purple and yellow. Hardly any of these items are extant.

[2] The shapes in Whieldon-style glaze are also found in enamelled and transfer-decorated creamware of the Ivy House period.

[3] Not the least of Wedgwood's financial problems was that of making a large enough fortune to marry his cousin Sarah.

[4] See 'Dry Bodies' p. 113 for further discussion on this question.

An order from a Dutch retailer dated 1763 requests Wedgwood to supply a number of wares of the old style, including agate, gilded black, enamelled salt-glaze and redware, as well as agate toys, 'pretty but not expensive'. It is clear that Wedgwood was perfectly prepared during this period to produce any wares he could sell. It is equally certain, however, that it was his intention only to produce these wares until such time as his business was considerable enough to enable him to put new experimental wares, especially improved creamware, into production.

The Ivy House Works were retained by Wedgwood until 1773. In 1764 he rented for £21 per year the Brick House at Burslem — known also as the Bell Works because the workmen were summoned by a bell instead of the usual horn. After this date only the 'useful' wares were produced at the Ivy House. Its function became subsidiary to that of the Brick House, and its production an extension of the larger factory's.

The Ivy House period, which engaged the five years from the termination of the partnership with Whieldon in 1759 until the opening of the Brick House Works in 1764, must be regarded primarily as the period of the green glaze, the cauliflower, the pineapple and the improved Whieldon-style wares. These are the first specifically Wedgwood wares, and for the collector they mark the emergence of the great potter.

PLATE I

The Wedgwood Jasper Colours.   A collection of cameos for box-top, buckle, and jewelry settings, all prior
to 1790

CHAPTER TWO

CREAM-COLOURED WARE 1760

CREAM-COLOURED WARE
1760

CREAMWARE, by the end of the eighteenth century irrevocably associated with the Wedgwood factory,[1] was, by tradition, anticipated about 1725 by an Astbury who, mixing marl with ground flint, produced a body which acquired a deep cream colour when fired. Before this, potters had whitened their wares by mixing flint with the lead ore used in glazing, and, in the seventeenth century, a cream-coloured clay was used to make moulded relief decoration for the redwares which were the staple Staffordshire products. Astbury subsequently improved his cream colour by careful preparation and blending of fine local clay with evenly ground flints. This early creamware, dusted with powdered lead ore, was fired at a lower temperature in the same kilns used in salt-glazed stoneware manufacture; its cream colour varied[2] and was inconstant, and its glaze was uneven in quality.

Creamware was produced by this technique until about the middle of the century, when Enoch Booth of Tunstall is credited with having introduced into the Potteries the technique of 'twice-firing'.[3] Through this innovation the possibilities of cream-ware were developed far beyond those of the attractive but limited salt-glaze to which it had till now been secondary. Whieldon further improved the ware by using calcined flint and clays from the west of England. Apart from the work in the development of creamware attributable to Enoch Booth and Thomas Whieldon, other potters, among them Warburton and Aaron Wedgwood, experimented in and improved the ware before Josiah Wedgwood began his manufacture of it in 1759–60. Through the period of his partnership with Whieldon, Wedgwood had experimented with it.[4]

At Fenton Vivian he was able to study thoroughly creamware manufacture, noting

[1] Although by 1774 more than a hundred potters in Great Britain were making it.
[2] The cream colour itself is due to the presence of iron as an impurity in the lead ore.
[3] The ware was by this method fired once to the biscuit state, then dipped in a suspended solution of lead ore, flint and pipe-clay, dusted with colouring re-agents, and fired again.
[4] The affair of Champion's Patent was certainly a delaying factor in the development of a near-white Staffordshire ware. Cookworthy's Patent, granted in 1768, monopolized the China clay and stone of Cornwall, and was assigned in 1774 to Champion of Bristol, who at once applied for an extension of patent rights for a further 14 years. The potters, led by Wedgwood, petitioned the House of Lords, and Champion's Patent was then amended to cover only transparent ware. Even so, it restricted Wedgwood in his experiments to achieve a whiter ware. [Continued at foot of next page

its peculiar problems in the dipping and firing, and remarking its possibilities in both decorative and useful applications. During the period of the Ivy House, he had little time to give to experiments which would not be immediately productive, but he bore the development of creamware constantly in mind.

Wedgwood's principal problem in creating this hygienic and adaptable ware was evenness and regularity of quality and colour. His early creamware has been described as varying 'from an extremely light primrose or straw-colour to the deepest saffron', and there were buyers for every tone in that considerable range. But the market for the ware could only be properly served if evenness of colour could be assured from firing to firing. Purchasers would lose patience with the ware, if, when they came to replace or extend their stocks, they found the new pieces different in colour from the original. Charming as this variation might be to contemporary collectors, to Wedgwood it was a disability to be made good as soon as possible. In 1768 he wrote to his office in London:

'With respect to the colour of my ware, I endeavour to make it as pale as possible to continue it *cream-colour*, and find my customers in general, though not every individual of them, think the alteration I have made in that respect a great improvement. But it is impossible that any one colour, even though it were to come down from heaven, should please every taste, and I cannot *regularly* make two cream-colours, a deep and light shade, without having two works for that purpose. Nor have I any clay to make with certainty a very light colour for tea-ware.'

Wedgwood's intention was to bring the creamware colour as evenly near to white as possible.

By 1780 Wedgwood was producing a fine white-glazed earthenware of the same body as creamware, but with the cream colour negated by an admixture of cobalt blue to the glaze. This new ware he named 'pearl'. The peak production period for pearlware is the first quarter of the nineteenth century, when it represents the factory's reply to the bone china manufacturers.[1] It is without difficulty distinguishable from creamware proper by its cold whiteness, and the tendency for the cobalt admixture to show as a distinct blue in corners and grooves where the glaze gathers. But in spite of its greater whiteness, pearlware found less general approval than creamware, and this is perhaps not surprising. One wonders, rather, why negative

Wedgwood formed a company with other potters for experimental work and to prevent monopolies, and Byerley, returned from America, became the company secretary. The association, however, quickly died.

Wedgwood wrote to Bentley in 1778, describing Champion's Patent as a 'cunning specification'. 'Poor Champion,' (he continues) 'you may have heard, is quite demolished. It was never likely to be otherwise, as he had neither professional knowledge, sufficient capital, nor scarcely any real acquaintance with the materials he was working upon. I suppose we might buy some *Growan stone* and *Growan clay* now upon easy terms, for they have prepared a large quantity this last year.'

[1] 'New Pearl White' was used for the Royal Jubilee service in 1809, the decoration being in orange transfer and coloured enamels. Following the success of this pearlware service, a number of services were commissioned in pearlware, decorated with armorial devices, and scroll and feather borders in gold and blue.

white should have been taken as a sign of perfection in ware. Certainly the soft cream colour, and the modestly elegant and perfectly balanced shapes which Wedgwood designed for the ware, are profoundly attractive to those who with Miss Meteyard abhor 'the ugly dead white hues of modern services'. Wedgwood's perfected cream-ware gains, through its gentler colour, tonal qualities deeply satisfying to the eye perceptive of the unassuming beauties of 'useful' ware.

No records exist of Wedgwood's early experiments with creamware, but the body used by him at the Ivy House is so like Whieldon's as to be indistinguishable other than by the shapes and glazes used. In fact, the cream body of the earliest Wedgwood period does not differ essentially from the best of Whieldon's creamware; yet even in these first years of his production Wedgwood must have been well-advanced towards perfecting the ware. In 1762 he presented Queen Charlotte with a caudle and breakfast set[1] with raised sprigs of flowers painted in natural colours by Steele and Daniell. In view of the importance which Wedgwood placed on the royal patron-age, it is unlikely that he would have made this presentation unless confident that his creamware was, at least, superior to that produced by any other potter. A reasonable inference is, therefore, that by 1762 Wedgwood was confident of his ability to produce a perfected creamware; but he was not yet capable of a large enough turn-out to make it generally marketable. The gift to the Queen (apart from its patriotism and loyalty) must have been recognized by Wedgwood for its promotional value to the ware in general. He is unlikely to have drawn such attention to goods which, demand for them being stimulated, his production could not supply.

Certainly by 1765, the year in which Wedgwood was first styled 'Potter to the Queen'[2] he was able to supply perfected creamware in the quantities its fast-growing

[1] This presentation is quoted by Miss Meteyard, drawing on Simeon Shaw, who describes the caudle set as 'made of the best cream colour and painted in the best style of the day. She suggests that the caudle service was 'most likely a sort of dejeuner or supper-tray, on which covered basins and spoons for caudle took the place of cups, saucers, and teapot, or plates and dishes.' Even if we allow for Shaw's often remarked inaccuracy, we are fairly safe in assuming that Wedgwood presented something of the sort to the Queen before 1765, in order to draw her attention to the new ware.

[2] Miss Meteyard states that Wedgwood was made Potter to the Queen in 1763, although she suggests that his business with the Royal Family was carried on through Lord Gower. In 1765 the Queen ordered a tea service but surprisingly, did not apply directly to Wedgwood, but to one of his neighbours from whom the commission (says Miss Meteyard) 'ultimately fell into Wedgwood's hands.' If Wedgwood was indeed the royal potter at the time it seems strange for him not to be directly approached with this commission. These confused stories may, however, be taken to indicate that between 1762 and 1765 Wedgwood set out to consolidate his position by becoming the royal potter, but that no clear patent was given to him. Wedgwood in effect became 'Potter to the Queen' by usage rather than formal arrangement.

Certainly in 1765 Wedgwood supplied: 'A complete sett of tea things, with a gold ground & raised flowers upon it in green, in the same manner of the green flowers which are raised upon the *Mebons*, so it is wrote but I suppose it should be *Melons* — The articles are 12 Cups for tea, & 12 Saucers, a Slop bason, sugar dish with cover and stand, Teapot & stand, spoon trea, Coffee pot, 12 Coffee cups, 6 prs. of hand candlesticks & 6 melons with leaves. 6 green fruit baskets & stands edged with gold.'

Afterwards the firm received regular orders for a wide range of items. A 1795 order lists:
'12 Milkpans,   6 Dog Pans,   Sundries,   3 Dog Pans,   18 Plates Green Ivy,   Silver Spout Teapot, 2 Teapots,   Jasper Vases and Gerandoles,   6 Plates Green Ivy,   2 Toy Tea Sets,   Sandwich Set.'

market demanded. From this date Wedgwood's creamware may be properly termed 'Queen's ware', and its great period considered to begin.

Queensware once perfected, its application and treatment had to be considered and developed. It is noteworthy that the caudle and breakfast set presented to Queen Charlotte were painted over relief. From the outset Wedgwood intended to develop decoration suited to Queensware, and valuing as he did the ceramic quality of his product, he determined that it should not be overshadowed by harsh colour, irrelevant motif, or pretentious embellishment. Suitabl decoration would underline the shapes, appropriate colours harmonize and relieve the cream body and fine glaze. Such decoration demanded extensions of both personnel and manufactory.

About 1770 Wedgwood arranged with Thomas Bentley[1] for the latter to open a workshop in Cheyne Row, Chelsea, and there many painters were engaged in the decorating of creamware. The list on pages 50, 51, while not at all complete, suggests the expense and trouble taken to develop borders and other styles suited to the new ware. These styles grew out of those same 'Etruscan' originals which inspired the Wedgwood shapes. The classical borders of leaves and berries, the Greek fret and key patterns, and the egg and tongue style found on the early vases, were taken as basic patterns. From them were developed the specifically English, largely florally derived patterns, recorded in the Pattern Book.

Of many of these styles (see list on pages 49, 50) there are no extant examples, although with the growth of collectors' interest in decorated creamware it is certain that more and more specimens will come forward. Due to long years of neglect of the 'useful' wares, most museum collections are singularly deficient in this most important field of Wedgwood's activity. For while jasper has always engaged the attention of enthusiasts, Queensware has remained the cinderella of Wedgwood wares, winning only in the past few years the approval and interest of ceramic connoisseurs. Throughout the past century and a half magnificent decorated services have been used to the point of extinction the world over, until, today, single 'potted pieces' in some of the early patterns are as rare as fine jasper portrait medallions, for many years the most sought-after of Wedgwood items.

The value of decorated creamware in its period is exemplified by the greatest of Wedgwood's achievements in this field, the Imperial Russian Service. In its undecorated state the service cost £51. 8s. 4d. When finally decorated, Catherine II paid about £3,500 for it, its manufacturing cost to Wedgwood being in the neighbourhood of £3,000. Although there are few specimens of the Russian Service outside Russia,[2] so important is it in the history of Wedgwood's creamware (for it established the fashion for it in high places), and so well does it show Wedgwood at work, it is

---

[1] The partnership was in the manufacture of *ornamental* wares; to be and maintain copartners or joint traders in the art mistery trade or occupation of making and vending ornamental earthen Ware', but was loosely applied to table wares requiring decoration.

[2] The most important are items painted with coloured enamels in Wedgwood Family collections.

worthwhile recounting the story of its commission and completion[1].

In 1768 Wedgwood wrote to his business associate Matthew Boulton:

'I have waited upon Ld. Cathcart, the Ambassador appointed for Russia, to bring about the plan we settled of introducing my manufacture at the Court of Russia. I laid before his Ldship in the best manner I could the great advantages which wod arise from such an introduction to a manufacture which might be rendered much more important that it had hitherto been thought capable of attaining to. The Ambassador, but particularly his Lady, came into my measures with the utmost readiness, and I am to get done a plate by way of specimen with the Russian Arms & an edging round the plate, both in gold burnt in, & this I must get done in town. His Ldship has now ordered a large service, plain, to take with him, and I must now desire you will by return of post let me know at what other courts in Germany or Europe you shd be most solicitous to have this manufacture introduced, & I will endeavour to get it done, & at the same time it shod be made known to the *Introducer* where the princes of the several states may be supplied with the same goods. Ld Gower will send a large Table and desert service, I believe, to Paris next week.'

So successful was Lord Cathcart, already an enthusiast for Wedgwood's work, that in 1770 Mr. Baxter, the British consul in St. Petersburg, was commissioned to instruct Wedgwood to make a dinner-service for the Empress, each piece to be painted with different views of British scenery, houses, and landmarks of interest. The service would be used in the palace of La Grenouillière, and though each piece eventually carried as a crest a green frog, it was originally suggested that a child and a frog be painted on the underside of items as a distinguishing mark.

Baxter first discussed the project with Bentley at the Cheyne Row workshop. Bentley informed Wedgwood of the commission, receiving the following reply:

23rd March 1773

'I have a score or two of Executorship letters, to finish & send off today, and have Mr. Gardner with me agreeing about the finishing of my works and some other buildings which makes me rather busy, but I must say a few words to you about this sd service for my Great Patroness in the North, which the Consul has been so obliging to bring me. Be so good to make my best compliments & thanks to him, & in the next place, if you please to accept a moiety of the honor & profit in finishing this very superb commission, for such I truly esteem it, it is very much at your service.

I suppose it must be painted upon the Royal pattern & that there must be a border upon the rims of the dishes & plates &c of some kind, and the buildings &c in the middle only. The Child & Frog, if they are to be all in the same attitudes, may perhaps be printed.

[1] Told at length in DR. G. C. WILLIAMSON's monograph *The Imperial Russian Dinner Service* published Bell, London, 1909 in a limited edition of 300 copies, and very scarce.

I have no idea of this service being got up in less than two or three years if the Landskips & buildings are to be tolerably done, so as to do any credit to us, & to be copied from pictures of real buildings & situations — nor of its being afforded for less than £1000, or £1500 — Why all the Gardens in England will scarcely furnish subjects sufficient for this sett, *every piece having a different subject*. I think Mr. Baxter shod be spoke to very particularly to know what expence he thinks it wod be prudent to lay upon the service, for he cannot but know than any sum almost may be expended upon this commn.

After you have settled that point if you could get the old plates, or the use of them for an impression from each of Stow Gardens &c. something clever might perhaps be done at a tolerable expence — What our hands can do in this business I do not know, you will try the likelyest, & get what other help you can, which you think necessary. I suppose this service is order'd upon the idea of the two services geting up by the King of Prussia which I suppose, have taken, or will take many years to complete. One with all the battles between the Russians & the Turks, drawn under his Majestys inspection & intended as a present you know to the Empress — & the other with all the remarkable views & Landskips in his Dominions, for his own use.

Suppose the Empress shod die, when the service is nearly completed, as it will be a very expensive business, it may not be amiss to mention something of the kind to the Consul.

One wod on the other hand avoid giving offence by overmuch caution. I will ask Mr. Sparrow what is necessary to be done to make an order binding upon the giver, & write you farther.

P.S. I want no more sd about the usefull ware in the Catalogue but just to let our frds know that it is continued as usual with various improvements that they may not think our whole attention bestow'd upon ornamts which you know some of 'em are much inclined to do.'

So concerned was Wedgwood for adequate surety for the enormous undertaking of the Catherine service (its importance as a promoter of interest in the 'usefull ware' is made clear in his postscript) that he returned to the question in a later letter:

27th March 1773

'I think we shod have some assurance that no revolution in the North shod affect the validity of the Consul's order to us. To paint a number of pictures which can only suit one particular situation, to the amount of one or two thousand pounds without any assurance of their being accepted farther than a verbal order which may be countermanded at pleasure, is rather too great a risque. And as these painting will enhance the value of the pieces so monstrously beyond the prices *Earthen Ware* Dishes & plates ought to bear; this alone, if there is not a thorough understanding of this circumstance with the Consul before the execution, may furnish a plausible excuse for rejecting the order when completed. Other causes, *many* other causes may have the same effect. The Death of the Empress, a revolution in Government or *ideas*, a War, or bad understanding with our Government. The Death or change of the present Consul, or even our offending him (a very possible chance, you know) may cause a countermand of this order, unless it be given in some way to make it binding. One wo^d on the other hand avoid giving offence by over-much caution.'

Bentley himself was perfectly prepared — so important did he consider the commission to Wedgwood and Bentley's business in useful ware — to act on it without personal advantage, and in such terms did he reply to Wedgwood. Wedgwood's answer makes it clear that whilst concerned at the risk involved in undertaking the Empress Catherine's commission, he had not the least intention of turning it down.

29th March 1773

'I am much obliged to my Dear Friend for his kind offers of assistance respecting the Russian service, but I do not see how I can do anything in it myself at this distance & when I can come to you is extremely uncertain, so that the whole burden must lie upon you, & how can I think of your having all the trouble, & sharing none of the profit? But if you think it cannot be kept distinct or have any other objection to its being a Partnership service, we must order it some other way, for I must insist on your sharing it with me in some way or other. One of my reasons for proposing it was that I thought it would furnish employment for Mrs. Wilcox & Mr.——I have not his name at hand he that paints & prints the outlines in the little Chamber, & perhaps Miss Isaacs might paint, or if printed, touch up the Boys & Frogs.

Do you think the subjects must all be from *real views*, & *real Buildings*, & that it is expected from us to send draftsmen all over the Kingdom to take these views — if so, what time, or what money? wo^d be sufficient to perform the one, or pay for the other. — As to our being confin'd to Gothique Buildings only, why there are not enough I am perswaded in Great Britain to furnish subjects for this service.

I think before we begin upon this capital work Mr. Baxter should give us some idea of the expense he would venture upon in the service, as it may be done to any value above £1500 or £2000, but I think not for less to do us any credit.'

The serious question of a price for the service had yet to be considered. On this matter Wedgwood had no intention of lowering his sense of the combined value of Wedgwood and Bentley's craftsmanship and the Empress's power.

5th April 1773

'The service might be completed for £400 or £500 but not *fit for an Empress's table* or to do us any credit at double that sum. The Dishes *very moderately* painted with real views & buildings cannot surely come at less than 20s. a dish, which will be £200 of the money and the plates at near half the price will almost make out the £500.'

The work (without 'assurances') began on 3rd April 1773, with Mrs. Wilcox and

James Bakewell painting the landscapes, and Nathaniel Cooper the borders. A week later Joseph Linley took over the borders while Mr. Wilcox worked with Cooper on the inner borders. These first items are probably the specimens in polychrome still in this country. By the time they were in hand Wedgwood realized the vast cost of a service so decorated. He writes:

9th Apr¹ 1773.

'I have some thoughts of paying a visit to My Dear Friend at Chelsea for a few days. — The plan talked of is to take my Wife to Lichfield & leave her with her Doctʳ a few days whilst I take this trip to Town (& if the weather is tolerable) on Horseback, that we may have a serious talk about this sd Table service, & I may have a peep at your first essays towards it. — Dare you undertake to paint the most embelish'd views, the most beautifull Landskips, with Gothique Ruins, Grecian Temples, & the most Elegant Buildings with hands who never attempted anything beyond Huts & Windmills, upon Dutch Tile at three halfpence a doz! — And this too for the first Empress in the World? — Well if you dare attempt & can succeed in this, tell me no more of your Alexanders, no nor of your Prometheus's neither for surely it is more to make *Artists* than mere *men*.

On the late journey I spent an evening at Knutsford with Mr. Stringer & looked at his Landskips & pictures, & told him something of the business we had in hand which I supposed would amount to 2000 views. He said it was a very arduous undertaking & must be a most expensive one if we did tolerable justice to the designs.

That there were very few Men in England clever at painting Buildings & on asking his opinion about the expence of painting each View upon our ware; he said it would be necessary to have each view sketched out from any that were now published by some good draftsmen, in order to adapt it to the piece to *take* & *leave* with skill & judgment &c. & that this woᵈ deserve half a Guinea for each design. The painting it upon the ware perhaps as much more; as to the borders, value of the ware, &c. he could say nothing to them but at a rough guess he supposed it could not be done for less than 3 or £4000 nor in less time than 3 or 4 years. — So far Mr. Stringer, I have now your good letter of 3ᵈ before me & am glad to find you have made a begining upon the service, by which you will soon find the value of these paintings better than from all the reasoning in the world, & to that tryal I resign all farther thoughts about it.'

Eventually, in order to bring the price of the service down it was decided to execute the painting in 'a rich mulberry purple.'[1] Even so, the service was to cost, Wedgwood insisted, far more than the Consul thought reasonable, for Wedgwood had not the least intention of allowing the Empress to eat off less than the best work his factory was capable of doing.

Working closely with Stringer, who was in charge of their artists, Wedgwood and Bentley put Samuel Armstrong on to the border decoration, and Ralph Unwin on to the landscapes, increasing the team of decorators to seven. In the process Wedgwood

[1] Some specimens were also painted in sepia.

further demonstrates his development procedure, as the following letter shows:

Etruria. 4th August 1773.

'Mr. Stringer has promis'd to get me a few views for the Russian service, but I do not expect more than perhaps half a doz. Do you think it would be worth while to ingage Stringer for a few months to paint & instruct our hands in London? Upon this plan I would bring him up to London — have a Camera Obscura with us, & take 100 views upon the road. There are many pictures, from real views of seats in the good houses in London — These must be come at as many as possible. Suppose a written advertisement asking that favor was put up in our Rooms. A Gentⁿ at Ld Gowers' gave me a good hint if it could be put into execution, which was to apply to Mr. Brown, tell him what we had to do, & that with respect to same no man in England was so much interested as himself in the execution of our plans. He could procure us a great number of designs, tell us who had the views of their pleasure grounds taken, & might lend us a hand to take others, & perhaps do more. I wish you could send me a good Camera Obscura, not too cumbersome, that I could take to the Neighbouring gentⁿˢ, seats here, as I find it will be in my power to pay some acceptable comptˢ in that way to some gentⁿ in our Neighbourhood.'

Other artists were brought in to work on the service. The account books for the period mention William Shuter, Thomas Major, John Boydell, and Jno Pye as having been employed on various parts of the work. Other artists travelled about the country making sketches, and the costs of the commission mounted day by day to the great concern of the Consul. But Wedgwood answered his complaints shortly: 'We cannot tell to a hundred pounds or two what the expense will be, and should therefore have some latitude in our agreement.'

Apparently a price had not yet been determined, and on this essential point Wedgwood eventually bypassed the Consul, and perhaps using the good offices of Lord Cathcart again, approached the Empress direct on the subject. The following letter makes it quite clear what the results of this representation were:

Trentham, 30th July 1773.

'I thank you for the good account from St. Petersburg. The Empress has again prov'd herself to be what we had before all the reason in the world to believe she was — a Woman of sense — fine taste, & spirit. — I will have some real views taken & send them to you, from Trentham — Keel, Lawton, Booth, Swinnerton, Shutboro', Ingestry, Etruria, & many other places. Pray have you Wilsons views from different places in Wales. If you have not Mr. Sneyd will lend them us.

The Consul should not talk of *doing them as much lower as we can* — If his Mistress heard him she woᵈ rap his knuckles — we could do them as much lower as he pleases but to do them in the manner the Empress wishes to see them; & as we (I mean the Consul & all of us) may receive due honor from the execution of the noblest plan ever yet laid down, or undertaken by an Manifactures in Great

43

Britain. — The price agreed upon is cheap beyond comparison with anything I know, & you will I make no doubt of it convince the Consul of it *in due time.*

There is another source for us besides the *publish'd views*, and the real Parks & Gardens. I mean the paintings in most Noblemens & Gentlemens houses of real Views, which will be sketch'd from by some of our hands at less expense than we can take real Views, but I hope prints may be picked up to go a great way or we shall be sadly off as they are to be number'd and nam'd.'

The service, when finally completed in 1775, consisted of 952 items painted with 1,244 scenes, the finest pieces being three ice pails which Wedgwood designed himself. Surmounted by a group of three women symbolizing Winter (Wedgwood described the pails as *glaciers*), they were intended as containers for creams and jellies. Many of the other potted pieces were based on Flaxman's designs, and the pictures which Dr. Williamson made in 1909 show the service to have been of extraordinary interest and quality. The sample plates and dishes decorated in natural colours, and which are on show to the public in the Wedgwood Museum collection, make an enthusiast long for a sight of the Service itself; still in Russia and insulated for the time being from the rest of the world.

Simultaneous with the development of freehand and border styles on creamware, fine quality transfer-decoration was developed to superb effect, the dark tones of the transfers displaying excellently against the cream ground, achieving a richness rarely equalled in the similarly decorated white porcelains of the period.

The earlier work in the field of transfer-decoration is by the firm of Sadler and Green in Liverpool, with whom Wedgwood began to deal about 1760, sending from Burslem large consignments of ware to their workshops. There the transfers were laid on, and the ware returned to Staffordshire for firing, although in the case of consignments intended for export, firing may have been completed in Liverpool. The colours used, apart from black tones showing a large variation, were browns, reds, yellow and a dull green. Subjects were landscapes of historical interest or in the style of Watteau, domestic subjects, commemorative themes, comic subjects, foliage, flowers and birds. The transfer decoration was sometimes subsequently overlaid with enamel by Wedgwood's decorators in Staffordshire.[1]

[1] A notable example is the beautiful pattern described as 'Shells and seaweeds'. 'Yes. I make no doubt Painting and Printing may exist together. I hope we shall do both in quantities both in Table and Teaware. Many patterns cannot be Printed, and these will employ the pencils. I had wrote to Mr. Green upon the first sight of the Shell patterns that they were coloured too high, and must be kept down — especially the green. Shells and weeds may be colour'd as chaste as any subjects whatever, and I hope we shall get into the way of it in time. But this pattern was intended chiefly for abroad, and foreigners in general will bear higher colouring and more forcible contrasts than we English.' (Wedgwood to Bentley, 1776.)

Wedgwood's interest in conchology is reflected elsewhere in his art. The flatter shells were copied for plates, while larger convoluted shells served as basins, baskets, dishes, and centrepieces. The well-known 'nautilus dessert service' appears in various styles, the earliest example simulating the pink and pearl-white shades of natural shell. A 'cockle shell dinner service', embellished with cockle shells in relief, and tinted in various shades of brown was also made, as well as many other items in the form of various bivalve shells used for serving shellfish, preserves and pickles.

Some of the early subjects laid on Wedgwood creamware were also used by Sadler and Green for the wares of other factories. But Wedgwood, as soon as his circumstances permitted, insisted on keeping the designs for his creamware exclusive, undertaking to supply the engravers with new subjects in considerable quantity, a fresh design for every dozen plates, and distinctive decorations for the principal potted pieces in every service. Wedgwood clearly appreciated the dangers implicit in Sadler's method of decoration. We find him writing to Bentley that:

'I have had a good deal of talk with Mr. Sadler, and find him very willing to do anything to improve his patterns. He has just completed a sett of Landskips for the inside of dishes, &c., with childish scrawling sprigs of flowers for the rims, all of which he thinks very clever, but they will not do for us. He is trying the purple, and thinks he shall manage it, and is willing to have a sett of the red chalk stile, or mezotint flowers, but thinks they can do them at Liverpool best. I am afraid of trusting too much to their taste, but they have promised to offtrace and coppy any prints I shall send them without attempting to *mend* or alter them. I have promis'd to send him the red chalk plates and a few prints of flowers immediately, and beg you will send him the plates, and pick out some prints of different size flowers to send along with them by the coach to Liverpool.'

Wedgwood's pedagogic tone indicates the degree to which Sadler was dependent upon his business, as well as the firmness of his ideas on the use of transfer styles.

The arrangement with Sadler and Green continued with the latter (who was the firm's surviving partner) until about 1784, when the irritation and inconvenience it gave Wedgwood to incur the expense of travelling his ware and jobbing out the decoration, was relieved by the establishment at Etruria of engraving facilities. From then on new designs for printed patterns, together with printed outlines and transfers intended to be filled in by the enamellers, were made in Wedgwood's own factory. An inventory made in 1787 when Thomas Wedgwood, a cousin and partner in the manufacture of 'useful' wares died, included a lengthy list of engraved plates in stock at that time, indicating the range offered by Wedgwood in transfer decorated ware.[1]

It was not surprising that in the space of a few years Wedgwood's creamware took the premier place in the world market for useful wares, displacing completely the heavier earlier pottery bodies. From Liverpool and London it travelled to all parts of the world. A letter from a Miss Hulton of Brookline, Massachusetts, to a Mrs. Adam Lightbody of Liverpool, dated 1772, indicates the demand for the ware;[2] and defines very well the restrained 'genteel' taste for which Wedgwood was catering:

'There is another commission which I am desired to beg the favour of you. That is a small crate of Staffordshire ware, if it be bought at Liverpool. I sent a

[1] This inventory appears to have been lost.
[2] One consignment to Amsterdam contained 50 fine quality dinner and dessert services principally of the pierced and gilt style.

crate of the Yellow Ware from thence which cost about £3 to my Brother and they are now demolish'd. My Sister liked them much and desires to have another crate, if I could trouble you to buy 'em, but she says if there's any new fashion or invention of Mr. Wedgwood of this kind of ware, that is approv'd, Shod prefer it to the yellow over again, but chuses the usefull & neat, rather than Ornamental, as they are for Common Service, therefore, nothing Gilt & no matter how few Tureens. . . .'[1]

This 'new fashion or invention' Wedgwood provided in infinite variety with his decorated Queensware. He intended it to combine perfection of body with quality of glaze; its excellence and variety of shape and decoration to give it a range never before known in pottery manufacture. Polite society the world over acknowledged and patronized the achievement.

For many collectors of Wedgwood the fusion of qualities Wedgwood achieved in decorated Queensware makes it the most exciting and satisfying of all the wares associated with his name. Certainly in its variety and colour, its elegance, modesty and balance, it embodies much of the best that was thought and felt in the eighteenth century.

NOTES TO CHAPTER TWO

Creamware is perhaps the most adaptable of all pottery bodies. From it Wedgwood made every conceivable type of useful ware including watering pots, milk pans, cream tubs, slabs and tiles, butter tubs, honey pots, twig baskets, moulds for pastry, jelly, ices, cakes and puddings, and 'bubbies' or artificial breasts for nursery use.

It is impossible to list all the patterns, decorations and shapes used in Wedgwood creamware, but the following is a broad representation which, it is hoped, will be more helpful to students than reproduction of a few individual items; for early creamware is identifiable by its shape and quality of decoration.

In early items the glaze often shows an oily, iridescent or rainbow effect when held at an angle to light; the body is light in weight; there is no crackle; items with border decorations are usually impress-marked in upper case, while earlier freehand and transfer-decorated items carry the lower-case mark: workmen's tool marks are commonly found on all items in the range.

Unmarked Wedgwood items may be distinguished from the similar Leeds cream-ware by the greenish glaze of the latter. Leeds items have deeper foot-rings, than do Wedgwood items which are flatter based.

(a) LUSTRE DECORATED CREAMWARE

After Scheffer, of the Stockholm Academy, had more completely described the nature of 'the Seventh Metal' or 'platina del Pinto' in 1752, platinum was extensively experimented with by the Staffordshire potters as a ceramic decoration.

[1] *Old Wedgwood*, 1944.

Wedgwood himself used platinum in various attempts to develop a silver decoration for basaltes. It often fired badly, emerging dull and grey-black in colour, although successfully fired pieces are found, decorated with various border patterns and centre motifs of interlocking 'vermicelli' lines, after silver chaising styles of the period.

The full development of platinum decoration in Wedgwood ware was left to the second Josiah, who used it on a large scale in the years 1805 to 1820 as an over-glaze decoration for pearlware.

The method used was as follows[1]: the platinum was precipitated from its solution in aqua regia, and thoroughly washed in water to remove acid traces. It was then put into suspension in an oily fluid prepared by dissolving sulphur and Venice turpentine in ordinary turpentine. Oil of lavender was added as required to thin the fluid to a working consistency. The preparation was then applied to glazed ware, which was re-fired at low red heat in a muffle-kiln as used in firing gilded wares.

The styles of lustre decoration used by the Wedgwood factory are none of them entirely original, but in the best examples they have great quality of lustre and colour.

(a) *Resist*: a pattern is traced in a 'resist' medium of honey or glycerine, and the platinum is laid over the entire surface of the piece. After firing, the platinum burnt over the resist surface can be washed and rubbed away. Both gold and silver resist were made.

(b) *Moonlight*: a lustre style in which gold, pink, grey, brown, and other colour stains are mixed to produce a marbled effect. Fine marbled or moonlight lustre items are often found in shapes and with handles identical to those used by Turner of Lane End and many such items unmarked are wrongly attributed to Wedgwood.

(c) *Purple*: rich purple ranging to soft pink lustre was extensively used on pearlware, largely on shell shapes and 'Nautilus' services. Sometimes the colour is enriched by 'shot' metal effects giving a golden iridescence to portions of the surface.

The purple lustre is found on many creamware items (although rarely on large pieces), many of them unmarked, yet by shape and style of lustre, certainly Wedgwood. But because of the general use of this style of decoration — the example of fine Moonlight by Turner, quoted above, must be one of many — it is unsafe to attribute lustre-decorated items to the Wedgwood factory unless they are impress-marked.

(b) CREAMWARE VASES

Although creamware was developed very largely as a body for useful wares, many fine vases were made in it, most of them in shapes also used in jasper and basaltes.

Often creamware vases were left undecorated, but enamel over-glaze decoration and gilding were both used.

The most distinctive style, however, in creamware vases is that described variously

[1] According to Burton.

as *variegated*, *marbled* or *crystalline*. The principle here was a simple imitative one. Colours were applied by splashing, and then combed or sponged together to simulate the patterns of natural polished stones. Metallic oxides were sometimes dusted on to the surface before being fired with similar results.

With these variegated styles, gilding of handles and rims was usual:

(a) *Agate*: a surface glaze in browns, greys, blues, greens, and fawns; both vases and cassolets (reversible candlesticks) were made, mounted on basaltes or white stoneware bases.

(b) *Marbled*: surface glaze in marbled colours, mounted on basaltes or white stoneware bases.

(c) *Granite*: mottled blue ground, similarly mounted.

(d) *Coloured glazes* with painted 'pebble' outlines, similarly mounted.

(e) *Porphyry*: a 'sprinkled' green glaze, often unmounted.

Most variegated creamware vases are of the Wedgwood and Bentley period, and are found with wafer, circular seal, and lower-case markings. Sometimes items are found with plain Wedgwood marks, and these probably pre-date the partnership.

The separately-made base and stem are usually secured to the body of the vase by a brass spigot with a circular turned termination. Pairs of vases and complete garnitures like those illustrated from the Tagg collection are extremely rare.

Solid variegated ware was also made, but without, one feels, the virtue of the earlier 'solid agate' which Wedgwood improved during his partnership with Whieldon.

(c) CREAMWARE BUSTS

The coloured creamware figures and busts, often attributed to Wedgwood because they are sometimes found impress-marked, should be rejected. Although Harry Barnard in 1924 gave, out of his great experience and understanding, excellent reasons why these items are almost certainly not from the Wedgwood factory, they are still frequently misnamed. Apart from their generally poor quality of modelling, and Wedgwood's known antipathy to this style of figure, the following reasons may be quoted for rejecting such items as products of Josiah Wedgwood's manufacture:

1. The body is of a heavy creamware, with a lead glaze which shows a distinctively blue tint; Wedgwood's creamware of the period has a yellowish tint.

2. A crackle unknown in period Wedgwood creamware is commonly found in these items.

3. Modelling is generally crude and colour garish, both being quite uncharacteristic of period Wedgwood ware.

4. The impressed mark WEDGWOOD in upper case is not of the same face and style found on true Wedgwood items.

48

PLATE II

Wedgwood Green Glazed Wares. A melon-style teapoy, and a solid green-glaze teapoy of a pattern also found in salt-glazed ware. The confiture dish in the shape of a bunch of grapes is a style still made by the factory. The leaf-shaped dishes are a typical application of the green glaze

5. Other Wedgwood manufacturing pottery in Burslem through the period were:

  Carlos Wedgwood, 1763
  Joseph Wedgwood, 1785
  Aaron Wedgwood, 1763
  John Wedgwood, 1763, Big House Works ⎫
  Thomas Wedgwood, 1763, Big House Works ⎬ partners
  Thomas Wedgwood, 1763, Churchyard Works
  Ralph Wedgwood, who afterwards went to Ferry Bridge, and was bankrupt
    in 1790.

  Any of these would have been entitled to use the impress mark, unless Wedgwood made arrangements with them to the contrary.

6. No references to such items have been found in invoices, notebooks or catalogues of the period.

(d) CREAMWARE PATTERNS

About 1767–8 Wedgwood put into use pattern boxes which were fitted with compartments lined with baize and held about seven plates of different patterns as samples. A typical pattern box in 1775 contained: 1 blue antique border, 1 purple antique border, 1 grape antique border, 1 purple shell edge, 1 green feather edge, and purple flower, 1 laurel border, purple, 1 blue ivy pattern.

  Wedgwood wrote (October 1774): 'The pattern-boxes of useful ware seem to be universally demanded from the idea they convey of the manufacture; and seem to be a part of the business particularly requiring attention.'

  The following is a list of principal patterns and borders developed and used 1774–1810, on ware potted in the following styles: Queen's (ribbed compartments on plate rims) Royal Ridges Lines Gadroon Feather Scallops Flutes Festoons Pierced (gilt decoration was highly popular).

Patterns and borders 1774

Printed bird	Etruscan green and black	Super purple flowers
Oat border	borders	Green oat-leaf border
Arrow	Marine pattern, purple	Blue lines
Green flowers	edge	Brown antique border
Green husks	Calico pattern and sprigs	Black antique music
Strawberry leaf	Enamelled shagreen	Red border
Black flowers	Etruscan green and black	Greek border
Blue shell edge	Green double lines	Shaded figures, purple
Green shell edge	Brown double lines	grounds
Ivy border, with sprigs	Laurel border	Red birds
Purple arrow heads	Green feather edge and	Calico pattern
Purple antique	flower	

49

Honeysuckle, in several
colours
Red Etruscan
Brown edge (inside)
Brown husk
Black and red spike
Deep rose colour, bell
drops

Red and black strawberry
leaf with drop
Pencilled landscapes
Light green, bell drops
Broad pea green and
mauve, brown lines
Blue convolvulus with
green leaves

Brown drop
Double laurel
Brown Etruscan
Dotted border
Green and shaded purple

Patterns added 1790

Red and black dotted
border
Green oat, blue lines

Green and black Etruscan
Green and purple grape
Brown strawberry leaf

Moss border

Brown drop husk, with green dots and lines, oak leaf, and brown acorns
Brown rose leaves and buds on pale green
Interlaced pattern, scarlet and green, with scarlet berries and gold edge
Flowing wreath of pale green berries and leaves
Interlaced ring work, green and gold
Pale green leaves on brown line
Brown edge, brown and scarlet berries with green leaves
Thistle border
Blue periwinkle, wreathed on a brown line
Rosebud border, coloured from nature
Helix ornamentation, black, gold, and vermilion
Green drop fringe, red tassels, brown edge, and dots
Diapers brown and blue, brown edge

Patterns added about 1810

Cottage   Naval   Autumnal leaf   Japan   Gilt peony   Chrysanthemum
Oriental

Other patterns

Egg-and-tongue
Drop husk
Grape and ivy leaf border

Green and brown wreath
Maeander
Dark brown parsley leaf

Vermicelli
Scarlet and brown antique

Bird's eye edging, royal blue and gold, with arms emblazoned
Longitudinal feather edge, gold, scarlet lines
Black spikes and rich flowers on wide scarlet edging, enriched with gold, crest in
centre.

(e) CREAMWARE DECORATORS

James Bakewell   employed at Brick House Works and Chelsea

W. Bourne	employed at Chelsea from 1770
John Boydell	employed on Russian Service
David Cooper	flower painter of considerable merit
Nathaniel Cooper	drew frogs on Russian Service
Crofts	partner of David Rhodes, started work at Newport Street
Coward	one of earliest painters employed by Wedgwood. Worked on Queen's Service 1765; permanently retained by Wedgwood at £200 per annum
Daniell	decorated caudle and breakfast set for Queen Charlotte
Catherine Dent	employed at Chelsea
Denby of Derby	encaustic enameller, worked Etruria and Chelsea
John Englefield	employed at Chelsea
Miss Glisson	employed in decoration of Russian Service and worked at Chelsea
Joseph Linley	employed at Chelsea
William Henshaw	employed at Chelsea
Thomas Hutchens	employed at Chelsea
Thomas Major	worked on Russian Service
William Mence	worked on Russian Service and employed at Chelsea
Ann Mills	employed at Chelsea
Miss Pars	employed at Chelsea
Jno Pye	worked on Russian Service
David Rhodes	employed at Chelsea, Wedgwood's principal enameller
John Roberts	employed at Chelsea
Grace and Ann Roberts	employed at Chelsea
George Seigmund	employed at Chelsea
William Shuter	worked on Russian Service
Thomas Simcock	employed at Chelsea
Joseph Simon	worked on Russian Service
George Simons	employed at Chelsea
Steele	worked with Daniell on caudle set for Queen Charlotte
Pierre Stephan	employed at Etruria
Stringer	employed to take views of English mansions, etc, for Russian Service
Christopher Taylor	employed at Chelsea
Mr and Mrs Wilcox	employed at Etruria and Chelsea
Ralph Unwin	started Brick House Works, moved to Chelsea
Wright of Derby	connected with Wedgwood over long period

(f) GEORGE STUBBS

Stubbs executed several wax moulds for Josiah Wedgwood, from which jasper tablets were made. These include *The Frightened Horse* (No. 236 in the 1787 Wedgwood Catalogue), and *The Fall of Phaeton*, of which the wax mould is still preserved in the Wedgwood Museum. 'He sleeps with us & wishes to employ some of his evenings in modelling a companion to his frighten^d horse, & has fixed upon one of his Phaetons for that purpose.' (Wedgwood to Bentley, 28th October 1780). Stubbs also designed nineteen cameo-size horses. Edward Burch is entered in Ledger M (p. 398) in the Wedgwood archives as having received sixteen shillings each for modelling horses, and this is taken to prove that Stubbs never modelled these items himself.

Other connections between Wedgwood and Stubbs are suggested by a large creamware punch pot in the Boston Museum of Fine Arts, decorated with transfers by Woollett of two shooting scenes by Stubbs. A mug with the same decoration is in the Schreiber Collection. These items suggest that Wedgwood acquired the rights of reproduction in transfer of some of Stubbs' work.

The most important connection, however, between Stubbs and Wedgwood, is the experimental work they undertook in the production of ceramic plaques. Stubbs, through his interest in enamelling, directed his attention, whilst working in the vicinity of Etruria, to parallel problems in ceramic painting. The results of his experiments were several paintings on ceramic tablets, most of them creamware, but some basaltes.

These tablets are all large, and presented considerable difficulty in the firing. Wedgwood wrote to London in 1777: 'My compliments to Mr. Stubbs, he shall be gratified but large Tablets are not the work of a day. We have been labouring at an apparatus for that purpose from the day I came down, & can report some progress.' In the following year he wrote: 'When you see Mr. Stubbs pray tell him how hard I have been labouring to furnish him with the means of adding immortality to his very excellent pencil. . . . You may assure him that I will succeed if I live a while longer.' By 1779 he was able to write that 'We shall be able now to make them with certainty.'

Ceramic plaques by Stubbs cannot have been produced in anything but the smallest quantities, although the exact number made is not known. The following are some extant examples of what is certainly the rarest of all decorated Wedgwood wares:

1782   Portrait of Stubbs on a white horse.   *Lever Gallery*
1794   Haymakers.   *Lever Gallery*
1794   Haycarting.   *Lever Gallery*
        (Two similar subjects, 'Haymakers' and 'Reapers' were also made and were in the Gilbey Collection until 1915, now in the National Gallery)
1791   Warren Hastings on a horse.
178?   Lion and dead tiger.   *Liverpool Museum*
178?   Portraits of Josiah and Sarah Wedgwood.   *Wedgwood Museum*

(g)   CREAMWARE RANGE — TRANSCRIPT OF 1774 CATALOGUE

A CATALOGUE

Of the different Articles of Queen's Ware, which may be had either plain, gilt, or embellished with Enamel Paintings, manufactured by Josiah Wedgwood, Potter to Her Majesty.

A SERVICE OF QUEEN'S WARE, of a middling size, with the lowest *wholesale Price*, at Etruria, in Staffordshire.

			s.	d.	£	s.	d.
	2 Oval Dishes	19 inches	2	6	0	5	0
	2 Ditto	17 ,,	1	6	0	3	0
	2 Round Dishes	17 ,,	1	6	0	3	0
	2 Ditto	15 ,,	1	0	0	2	0
	4 Oval Dishes	13 ,,	1	0	0	4	0
	4 Ditto	11 ,,	0	8	0	2	8
	4 Ditto	11 ,,	0	5	0	1	8
	4 Round Dishes	11 ,,	0	5	0	1	8
	4 Covered Dishes	—	2	0	0	8	0
Design 3, 24, 27	2 Terrines for Soup	—	7	0	0	14	0
Design 13	2 Sauce Terrines		2	0	0	4	0
Design 10, 11, 12	4 Sauce Boats		0	5	0	1	8
Design 25	2 Salad Dishes		1	4	0	2	8
Design 6 and 33	6 Salts		0	4	0	2	0
	2 Mustard Pots		0	4	0	0	8
	4 Pickle Dishes		0	3	0	1	0
	6 Dozen Flat Plates		2	6	0	15	0
	2 Dozen Soup ditto		2	6	0	5	0

This service plain, No.   comes to   £3 17 0

The same enamelled, according to the Patterns No. .

Ditto   Ditto .   .   .   .   .   .   No.

Ditto   Ditto .   .   .   .   .   .   No.

Ditto   Ditto .   .   .   .   .   .   No.

N.B. Any of these Articles may be left out, or changed, as is most agreeable; or others may be ordered from the following Catalogue, and the Price will vary accordingly.

Besides the Articles in a Common Table Service, the following may be had, if required:

Covers to all the Dishes, oval and round.

Dish Drainers to ditto,   ditto.

Design 35   Root Dishes, with Pans to keep them hot; *a* being the Bason for hot water; *b* the Dish for Peas, &c. &c., which takes off at *c*; *d* the Cover, which takes off at *e*.

Design 8   Gravy Cups, with Water Pans; the Part *a* contains the hot water, which is put in at the opening *b*.

Design 4	Covered Dishes, to stew or keep a Dish of Meat hot.
Design 18	Soup Dishes with Covers.
	Soup Dishes, oval and round, from 18 inches diameter to 12 inches.
	Dishes for Water Zootjes (Dutch Fish).
	Herring Dishes, single or double.
	Ice pails of different sizes, for Bottles of Wine and other Liquors.
	Pickle Stands of different kinds.
Design 17	Large Dish, which contains five small pieces, *a*, *b*, *c*, for Pickles of different kinds.
	Leaves and Shells of different kinds.
	Plats de Menage; or Epergnes for the Middle of the Table.
	Egg Baskets, to keep boiled Eggs hot in water.
Design 26	Egg-cups, with or without Covers.
Design 19	The same for poached Eggs.
Design 22	Oil and Vinegar Stands, containing from two to six Cruets.
	Egg Spoons.
Design 9, 14 & 15	Table Candlesticks of different Patterns, from 9 to 14 inches high.
	Bread Baskets, round and oval.
	Cheese Toasters, with Water Pans.
	Oval and round Potting Pots.
	Pudding Cups, oval and round, of different sizes.
	Shapes for Blanc-mange, great Variety.
Design 20	Asparagus Pans; six or more are put upon a round Dish.
Design 16	Monteths, for keeping Glasses cool in water, two sizes.
Design 7	Cuvettes, ditto.
	Cheese Plates, different sizes.
	Beer Mugs and Jugs, with or without Covers, different sizes.
Design 2	Large Soup Ladles.

DESSERT SERVICES, CONSISTING OF

	Plates.
	Compotiers of various Forms, Patterns, and Sizes, the Prices in Proportion to the above Plates.
Design 1 and 28	Fruit Baskets.
Design 32	Fruit Bowls with Covers.
	Cream and Sugar Bowls, various Forms, Patterns, and Sizes.
Design 30, 31	Sweet-meat Baskets.
Design 21	Croquants or Sweet-meat Dishes.
Design 5	Glacieres of different Sizes, in four Parts — *a* being the Cover

which takes off at *b*; *c* a Part which contains the Ice, and takes off at *d*; *e* the Bason which contains the Ice-Creams, which falls into the Part *g*, as shown by the dotted line *hh*, and leaves a space at *g*, to contain Ice at the Top. The handle *ii* is fixed to the Inside of the Cover *c*, by which Means it serves to lift off the Covers *a* and *c* both together when the Vessel is brought to Table.

Design 23 — Ice-Cream Cups and Covers.
Ice-Cream Bowls.
Strawberry Dishes and Stands.

Design 34 — Custard Cups, different Forms.
Tartlets.
Dessert Spoons.

COFFEE, TEA, AND CHOCOLATE SERVICES COMPLETE; WITH TEA KETTLES AND LAMPS

Water Plates with Covers to keep toast and butter hot, three sizes.
Gondolas for dry Toast.
Butter Tubs and Stands, oval and round.
Dejeurners, for one, two, or three Persons.

MISCELLANEOUS ARTICLES

Wash-hand Basons and Ewers, several sorts.
Shaving Basons,   do.
Punch Bowls, different sizes.

. . . .

. . . .

Spitting Pots.
Sauce Pans for Cooking, that will bear a Charcoal Fire.
Night Lamps, to keep any Liquid warm all night.
Table and Toilet Candlesticks, with extinguishers.

The Proprietor wishing to render his Manufacture as useful as possible, will gladly receive any instructions or particular designs from those who please to honour him with their commands, which he will endeavour to execute with the utmost attention.

(h) CREAMWARE SHAPES, 1817

William Blake drew and engraved the figures illustrated (14–29) for the Wedgwood firm in 1816, the date being determined by a watermark on the paper of one of four proofs in the Print Room of the British Museum.

Blake is said to have executed the engravings of the Portland Vase which were included in Erasmus Darwin's *Botanic Garden* published in 1791, but this is not certain. In any case he would have been commissioned for this work by the book's publisher, Joseph Johnson, and not by the first Josiah Wedgwood. Blake's friend Frederick Tatham wrote:

> 'Mr. Flaxman introduced Blake to Mr. Wedgwood. The Designs of the Pottery were made by Mr. Flaxman and engraved by Blake for some work. Wedgwood's last Sale of Pottery was about 35 or 37 years ago when I purchased several specimens. These were white that I purchased and were of very elegant shapes, some too elegant for use.'

The designs referred to have been attributed to the years 1781–3, but details of them have not so far come forward.

The Queensware patterns illustrated here have therefore, added interest, since, being signed by Blake, they are the artist's only proven connection with the Wedgwood firm.

CREAMWARE
AND
DRY BODY SHAPES

Pl. 1.

1   Creamware Shapes from the 1790 Catalogue
Designs 1, 2 and 3

2   Creamware Shapes from the 1790 Catalogue
Designs 4, 5, 6, 7 and 8

Pl. 5.

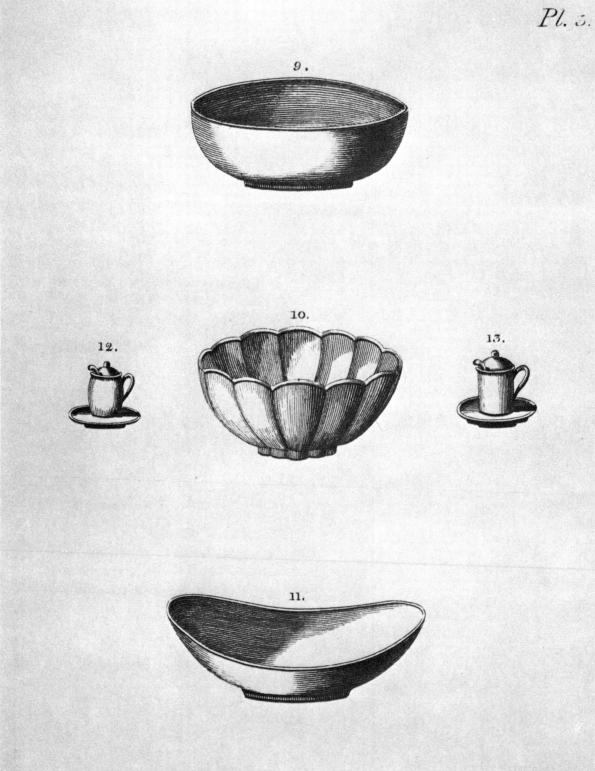

3   Creamware Shapes from the 1790 Catalogue
Designs 9, 10, 11, 12 and 13

4   Creamware Shapes from the 1790 Catalogue
Designs 14, 15, 16, 17, 18, 19, 20 and 21

Pl.5.

5   Creamware Shapes from the 1790 Catalogue
Designs 22, 23, 24, 25, 26, 27 and 28

6   Creamware Shapes from the 1790 Catalogue
Designs 29, 30, 31, 32, 33 and 34

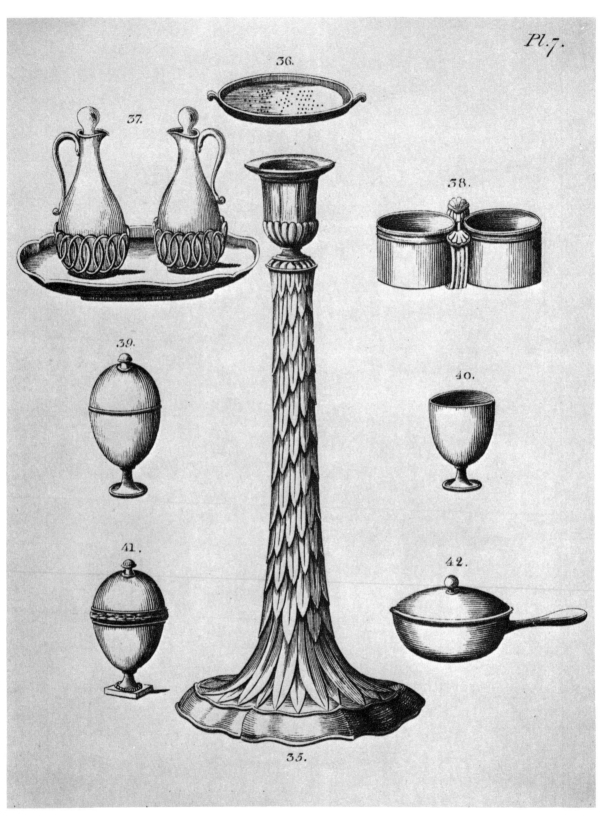

Pl. 7.

7   Creamware Shapes from the 1790 Catalogue
Designs 35, 36, 38, 39, 40, 41 and 42

8   Creamware Shapes from the 1790 Catalogue
Designs 43, 44, 45 and 46

Pl.9

9   Creamware Shapes from the 1790 Catalogue
Designs 47, 48, 49, 50 and 51

10   Creamware Shapes from the 1790 Catalogue

Design 52

Pl:11.

11   Creamware Shapes from the 1790 Catalogue
Designs 53, 54, 55, 56 and 57

58

_Pl._ 12.

59

63.

62.

60.

64.

65.

61.

12 Creamware Shapes from the 1790 Catalogue
Designs 58, 59, 60, 61, 62, 63, 64 and 65

13   Creamware Shapes from the 1790 Catalogue
Designs 66, 67, 68, 69, 70, 71, 72, 73, 74, 75, 76, 77, 78, 79 and 80

14 Creamware Shapes, 1817
Engraved by William Blake

15   Creamware Shapes, 1817
Engraved by William Blake

16   Creamware Shapes, 1817
Engraved by William Blake

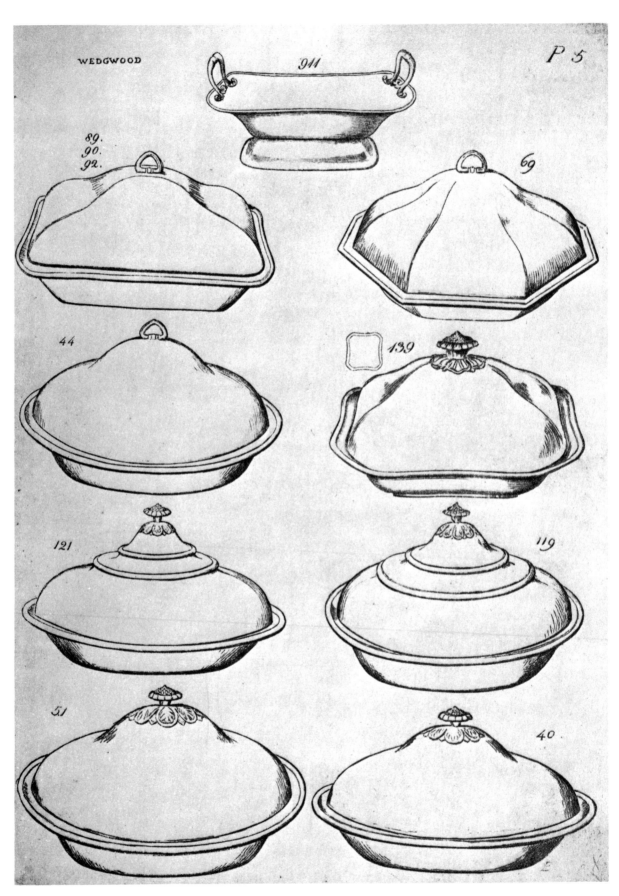

WEDGWOOD 911 P 5

89.
90.
92.

69

44

139

121

119

51

40

17 Creamware Shapes, 1817
Engraved by William Blake

WEDGWOOD

P 6

889

888

160

891

114

120

112

115

18 Creamware Shapes, 1817

Engraved by William Blake

19   Creamware Shapes, 1817
Engraved by William Blake

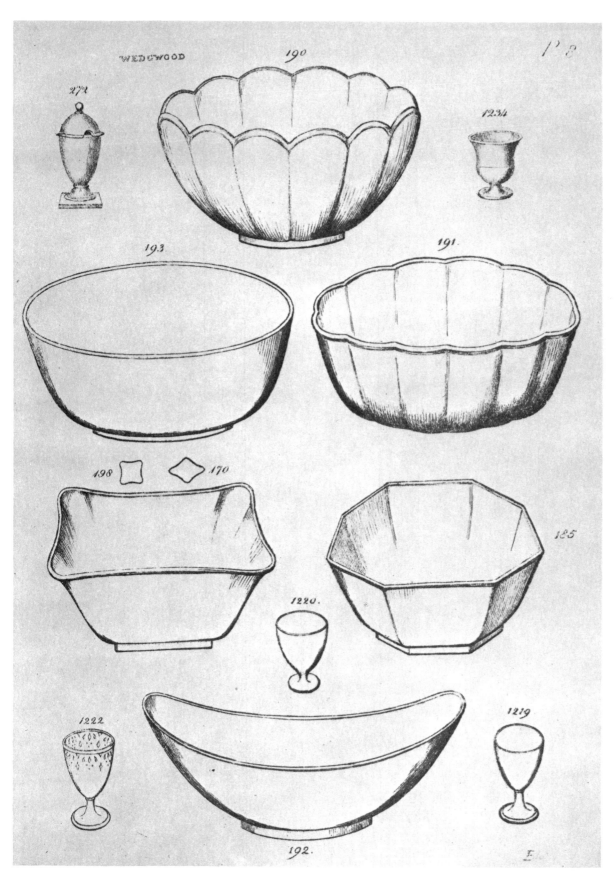

20   Creamware Shapes, 1817
Engraved by William Blake

21   Creamware Shapes, 1817

Engraved by William Blake

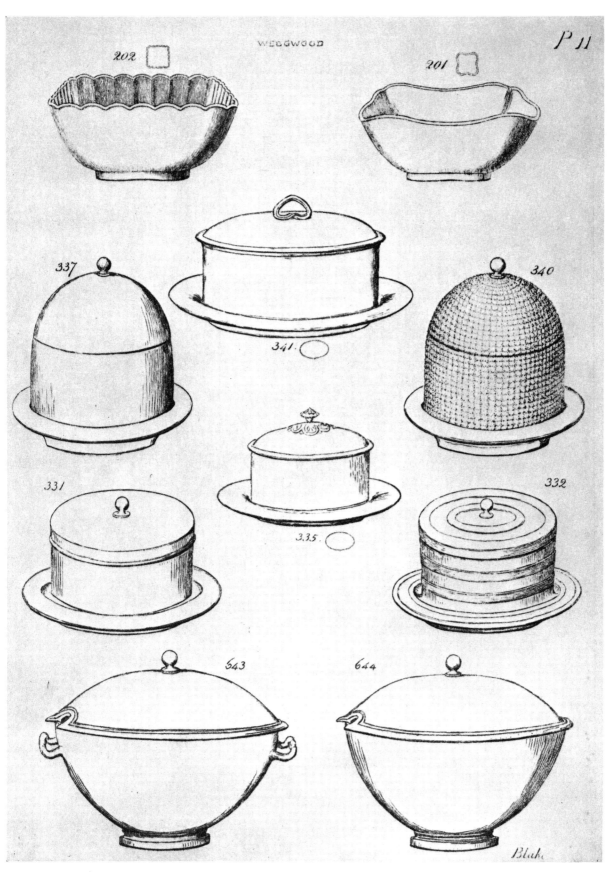

22   Creamware Shapes, 1817

Engraved by William Blake

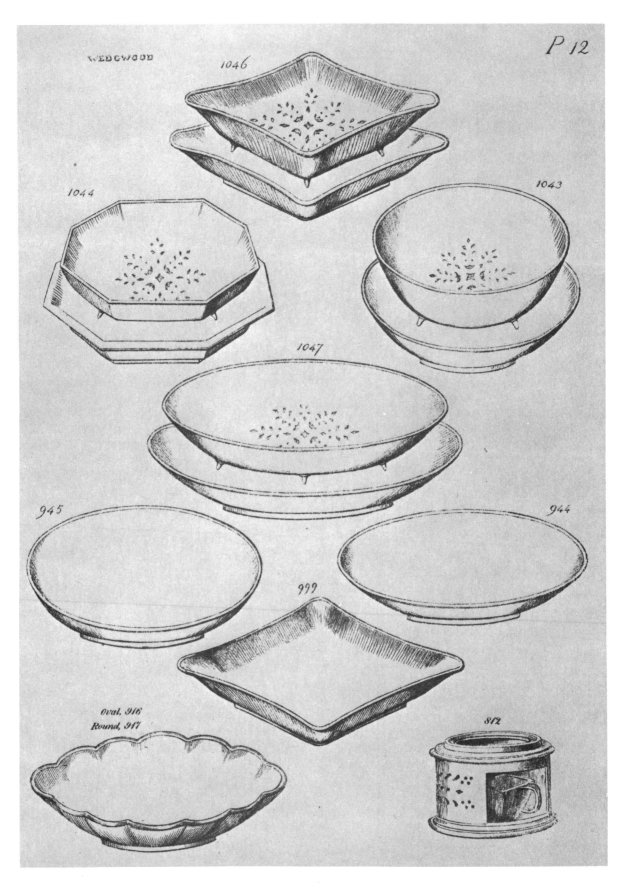

WEDGWOOD

P 12

1046

1044

1043

1047

945

944

999

Oval. 916
Round, 917

812

23   Creamware Shapes, 1817
Engraved by William Blake

24   Creamware Shapes, 1817
Engraved by William Blake

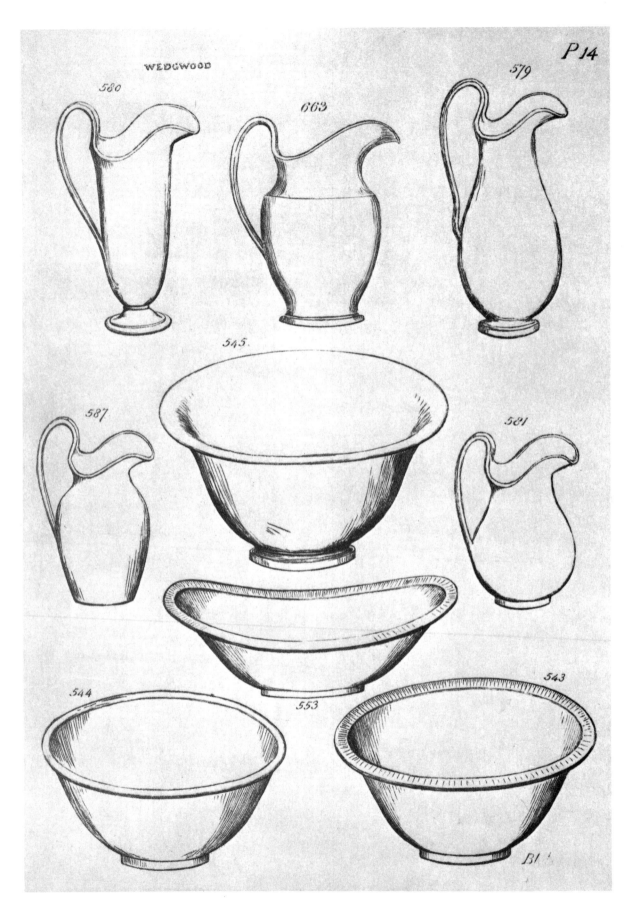

WEDGWOOD

580   663   579   P 14

545

587   581

553

544   543

25   Creamware Shapes, 1817

Engraved by William Blake

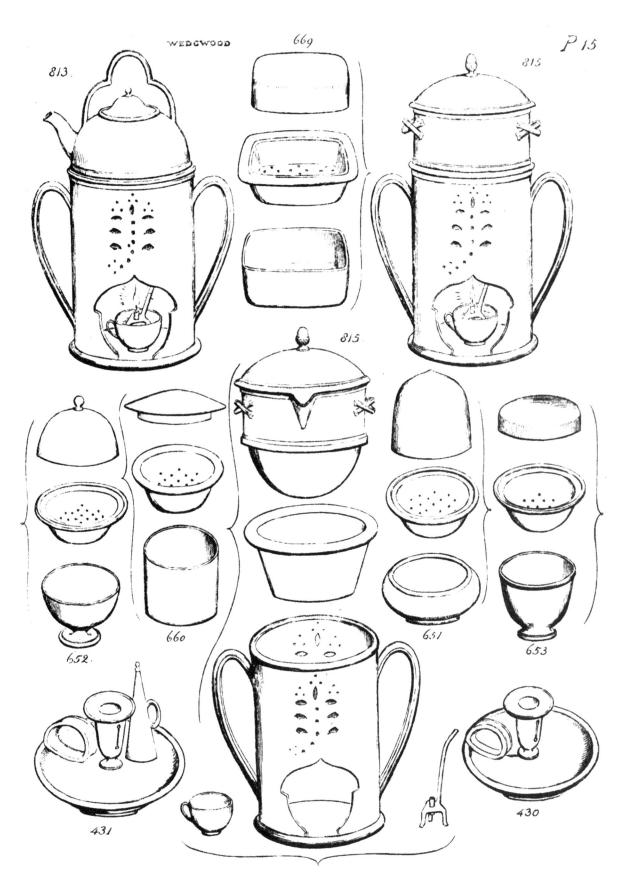

813.

815.

815.

652. 660 651 653

431 430

26   Creamware Shapes, 1817
Engraved by William Blake

27 Creamware Shapes, 1817

Engraved by William Blake

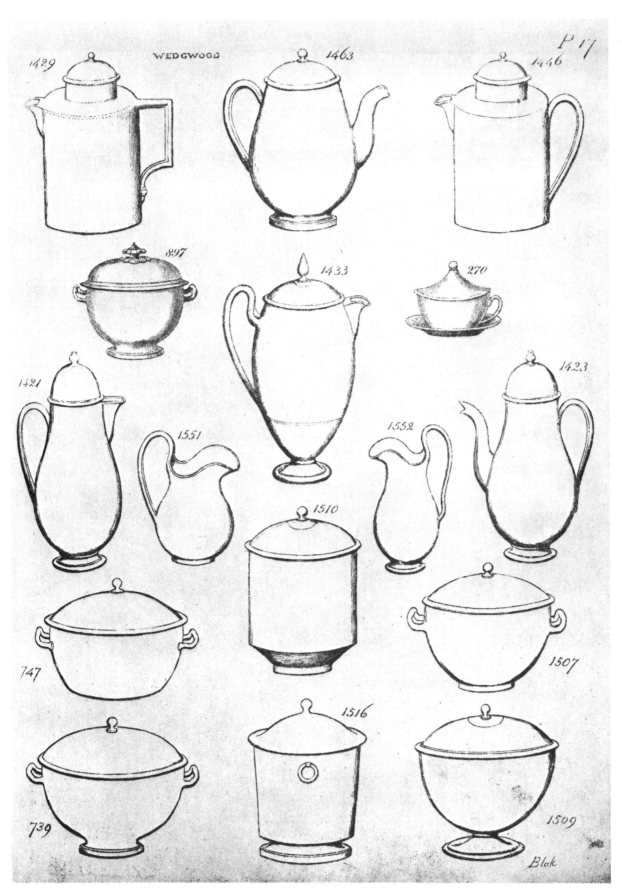

28   Creamware Shapes, 1817

Engraved by William Blake

29   Creamware Shapes, 1817

Engraved by William Blake

There are all the other pieces to make up complete
sets with the above Teapots.

Il y a aussi toutes les autres pieces pour les Services
quoiqu' on n'a figuré que les Théieres.

In one color as drab or cane or white,
and in 2 colors as cane & blue
or drab & white

vase & cover
Blue with white bassreliefs

958
Jug

Garden pot & stand

43

Green & white hoops
2 3 4 5 6 inches
2 3½ 6 9 9/

4 5 6 7 8 9 10 inches
5/6 6/9 7/9 9/ 10/6 13/ 15/

leafage Jug

Garden pot & stand
Brown & white fluted & honeysuckle
or Buff & white fluted & foliage

934
Flower vase

In drab, cane, or white
No 4 6 8 9 10
7/ 1/6 8/ 9/ 8/

cane blue bassreliefs
drab white bassreliefs

92
Flower vase

2 3 4 5 6 ins
3½ 6 9 1/ 1/3

3½ 4 5 6 inches
1/3 1/6 1/9 2/3

cane blue basfs on
drab white basfs

3½ 4 5 6 ins
1/3 1/6 1/9 2/3

Mortar & pestle

384
Flower vase

Flower basket
749

Inches 2 2½ 3 3½ 4
Price 8 10 1/ 1/3

4½ 5 5½ 6 6½ 7 7½ 8/9
1/6 1/9 2/3 2/9 3/ 3/3 3/9

9 10 11 12 inches
4/6 6/ 7/6 9/ 10/6 price

3½ 4 5 6 7 8 9 10 ins cane blue bas
1/3 1/6 1/9 9/3 3/ 3/6 4/6 6/6
2/6 3/ 4/6 4/ 6/ 8/ 9/6 11/ blue white

2½ 3 3½ 4 ins
1/9 2/ 2/9 2/3 4/6 cane blue basreliefs
2/ 4/6 2/9 3/ 5/6 blue white ditto

31 Dry Body Shapes from the 1817 Catalogue

CHAPTER THREE

THE WHITE BODY
1773-1796

THE WHITE BODY
1773-1796

(a) Waxen biscuit, 1774

(b) Jasper, 1776

IN order to exploit the market for decorative wares in the neo-classical taste, Wedgwood required a body with lapidary imitative possibilities. The Graeco-Roman objects of contemporary admiration were made of coloured glass or polished natural stone. To emulate these materials the new body should be white, capable of tinting to almost any required colour, and hard enough to be lapidary-polished after firing. It would probably be, therefore, a highly fired porcellaneous biscuit material; but the composition had yet to be invented.

Wedgwood worked throughout 1773–4 to the end of developing such a white body. His experiments were with white 'spars' and 'earths', many of them hitherto not used in pottery making. Particularly, Wedgwood experimented with two barium spars, of which the rarer was the carbonate (commonly called witherite); the other, the sulphate, is found in good quantity as a gangue of the lead ore mined in Derbyshire and the Peak district. Miners called this sulphate of barium, 'heavy-spar' or 'cawk'. Wedgwood refers to both spars as 'baryta' or 'spath fusible', and because of his early chemical confusion found their handling perplexing. In July 1774 he wrote to Bentley:

> 'M(oor) Stone,[1] & Spath fusible are the two articles I want, & several samples I have of the latter are so different in their properties that no dependence can be had upon them. They have plagued me sadly of late.'

He was 'plagued sadly' not only by the difficulty of obtaining requisite materials. ('I must go to Derbyshire myself in search of the Spath fusible,' he wrote, and travelled as far as Anglezark, Lancashire, to find it.) The materials once obtained, reacted differently to firing, emerging from the kiln in colours varying from white to saffron, and in consistency from that of glass to that of pipe-clay.

Also known as 'Growan' stone, a material on the use of which Champion had a patent.

Eventually Wedgwood found that the elusive fusible spath was not essential. 'I believe I shall make an excellent white body and with absolute certainty, without the fusible Sparr,' he wrote in September 1774; an important development commercially, for if the 'white body' was to be generally marketable it was necessary for it to be made from easily available sources.[1] The same month Wedgwood was able to inform Bentley that, 'From several late series of experiments I have no reason to doubt being able to give a fine white composition any tint of fine blue.' From this suite of experiments he was able to send his partner some small cameo and intaglio items in various blue and marbled, polished and unpolished, styles. 'These first seedlings,' he called them, 'which I have no doubt will in time become most beautiful plants.'

Wedgwood's optimism was justified, for by the end of the year he could record the discovery of 'A fine white terra-cotta of great beauty and delicacy.' This biscuit was subsequently defined by Wedgwood as his 'waxen' white body.

In 1776 he describes the invention of a finer body still: 'A fine white artificial *jasper*, of exquisite beauty and delicacy, proper for cameos, portraits and bas-reliefs.'

In the sixth and last edition of Wedgwood's *Catalogue* (1787) these two white bodies are described thus:

(a) 'White porcelain biscuit, with a smooth wax-like surface, of the same properties as the basaltes except in what depends on colour.'

(b) 'Jasper — a white porcelain biscuit of exquisite beauty and delicacy, possessing the general properties of the basaltes, together with that of receiving colours through its whole surface, in a manner which no other body, ancient or modern, has been known to do. This renders it peculiarly fit for cameos, portraits and all subjects in bas-relief; as the ground may be made of any colour throughout, without paint or enamel, and the raised figures of a pure white.'

It is important to realize that jasper was one of two white bodies which Wedgwood had by this time in regular production. The earlier 'waxen' body is densely opaque, white, hard and waxen in finish, and not as fine in quality as jasper proper. The jasper body is highly porcellaneous and often translucent; it usually appears to be intensely white, although Wedgwood himself wrote that: 'There are two kinds of white jasper — one a bluish, the other a yellowish tinge. The latter is its natural colour, the former is produced by a very little blue.' By 1776 Wedgwood considered that he had the vagaries of jasper entirely within his control, although he continued improving it, in hardness especially.

[1] The formula for jasper (published by Sir A. H. Church in 1903) was as follows:

Sulphate of barium (cawk)	59
Clay	29
Flint	10
Carbonate of barium (witherite)	2

William Burton, who was chemist at Wedgwood's for five years, describes the jasper body as 'finely divided barium sulphate with the addition of the smallest possible amount of clay.' The Derbyshire *baryta* sources, therefore, were of paramount importance in the making of jasper commercially.

The white body was quickly put into production, and from 1774 became a principal charge upon the turnout of Wedgwood's manufactory. On 1st January 1775 he wrote to Bentley:

'I am glad to think that the "white body" is of sufficient fineness — and have no reason to doubt of being able to continue it so. . . . The blue body I am likewise absolute in of almost any shade, & have likewise a beautiful Sea Green, and several other colors, for grounds to Cameos, Intaglios, &c., & shall be able to make almost any of our Cameos in figures from the Herculaneum size to the least Marriage of Cupid &c. & in heads from Peter the great to the smallest Gem for Rings, of the blue, & other color'd grounds, with the Figures & Heads in our fine white composition.'

This letter is of considerable interest, indicating as it does the speed with which Wedgwood could follow a period of experiment with production. For him, means of production and marketing were always a part of the experiment. A ware once discovered was, at the same time, prepared for manufacturing.

The jasper of this first period was used only for making cameos, seals, and small portraits, for the body had not yet been sufficiently investigated for larger masses to be fired with safety. The larger tablets and bas-reliefs, which were to be so superb a feature of the Wedgwood and Bentley period, had still to be developed. As for vases and tablewares, candlesticks and plant-pots, these were not to be realized before Bentley's death in 1780; although during his life jasper bases and stands were made, so that the larger items were well in sight.

By 1776, however, the production of the smaller range was complete and Wedgwood was able to report:

'I believe I can now assure you of a conquest, & a very important one to us. No less than the firing of our fine Jasper & Onyx with as much certainty as our Basaltes or Black Ware. We had about 8 doz. of heads all fired this new way, which I had tried a few times before with so much success that I ventur'd to put the above qu.ty to the test all at one firing, & they were every one good, except a few accidents in cracking, & scarcely any of them, but in respect to firing they were perfect, & the two bodies, blue & white agree perfectly together, &, as I manage them now, it cannot be otherwise. So I am fully perswaded this new Art, which I have more & more reason to believe will be a very capital one to us, is completed, & brought to perfection, & I heartily give you joy of this last discovery which has given the finishing stroke to the Art.'

The production of jasper continued through the year, with growing success. Wedgwood writes that he has: 'drawn more fine Jasper yesterday & not a single piece discolor'd, blister'd, or shewing any tendency to either of those disorders, so that I may now surely be confident of our being absolute in respect to firing this delicate substance.'

But jasper remained capricious — 'I have nearly managed my whimsical Jasper

93

Composition,' wrote Wedgwood a little after expressing renewed confidence in his conquest of it. In July 1776 he assured Bentley who was worried by the rumour that the jasper secret was out, that:

'The boast of my Neighbour, that he had found it out is idle — I would as soon believe he had discover'd the Philosophers Stone — Besides — If I was to give him the rec.ᵗ, it would half ruin him, & quite tire him out before he could make any-thing of it — but the R-Antᵒ¹ is made at the first essay. Everybody can make that colour, & composition, but nobody, besides W & B can make Jasper.'

In spite of Wedgwood's continued confidence, much early jasper contains firing blemishes, or colour 'bleeding'. This latter fault Wedgwood describes thus:

'In some things the blue shade which our ground is so apt to cast through the thin parts of the white, may be of advantage to the subject, as in the Armour by the side of the conquer'd Province — Any parts of Drapery which requires to be thrown back, or other apendages to the Figures — But when the naked part of the Figure is penetrated with the color of the ground, it is generally injurious — See the poor Queen's Nose, & many other Cameo's.'

The common question of whether the dark or the light blue jasper is the earlier is another which Wedgwood can best answer:

'The risque is the same with one color as another, only in respect to staining the white a middle tint for the ground will stain the white less than a full color'd ground. But you told me in a former letter that nobody bought a pale blue ground if a full color'd one lay near it, which induc'd me to attempt a deeper color, & the white has suffered by it.'

Clearly he experimented with and developed both colours at the same time; they are variations in tint not in body, although the dark ground was the more difficult to control:

'Black blue grounds are what I have been attempting a long time, & have some-times succeeded but much oftner miscarried; though both good, & the bad have been of the same mixture oweing to some differences in the fire which I cannot yet ascertain, or command. I shall pursue the object, as far as Cameos & Intaglios, for Rings, but to reconcile our Black Body, in Vases, to admit of an union with the Jasper in Bassrelief Figures of pale blue, is an arduous attempt, to say the least of it. I can only observe upon this subject that there is not saying what may, or may not be done: not even after all the attempts we have made may have failed.'²

---

¹ Rosso antico.

² The 'union' of jasper and basaltes did, in fact, fail. Other colour grounds were, however, splendidly developed. Green, black, yellow and lilac, were made, but the often described colours 'peach', 'pink', 'coffee', 'sage', and so on, do not exist as manufacturing colour groups. They are entirely variations on basic colours provided by oxides being added to the white body in varying quantities. These variations however, were never completely controllable, so that it is useless and entirely unscientific for enthusiasts to create 'rare' colour groupings for variations which they happen to possess. As Burton remarks: 'I think

[Continued at foot of next page

The output of the early jasper period remains principally, the smaller cameo items. Tablets were proving difficult to make; the patient Wedgwood writes: 'The tablets I do not despair of, but that must be a work of time.' Late in 1776 he wrote again on the question of tablets:

'I have sent a Jasper Tablet, short fired, that you may see what state we are in; we have done with the cracking which teized us so much in the former compositions and only want a proper fire to make us absolute. When I tell you that the fire this Tablet has gone through would be sufficient for the Statues, & too hot for the small ring Cameos, You will perceive some of the difficulties we labor under in having a proper fire for this delicate composition. However I shall persevere, & hope, as all projectors do you know to Conquer.'

Eventually Wedgwood and Bentley did put out jasper tablets, and they are without doubt the rarest and finest in this field of Wedgwood ware.[1] But they must be accounted among the very scarcest of jasper, for their period of production is certainly no more than three or four years.

The distinctive characteristics of jasper have been often described. Certainly, no-one with experience in handling it is likely to make very serious mistakes in the dating of fine jasper[2] of the period which ends with the death of Josiah Wedgwood in 1796. Yet, because the manufacture of one kind or another of jasper has continued to the present day, both collectors and dealers without much experience in its handling find the ware difficult to date. The following characteristics are observable in the period ware:

1. *Surface*: even and symmetrical. Very smooth and free of wave or scouring marks and crazing. Often shows bleeding of the colour ground. Small firing cracks, especially in larger items.

2. *Relief*: high detail and accuracy in even the smallest gems, with considerable variation in delineation of folds, etc. The bleeding of the blue ground often adds to the delicacy of the cameos, for Wedgwood capitalized what would otherwise have been a fault, by careful selection of subjects.

3. *Undercutting*: 'undercutting' is a process which precedes firing. In the 'cheese-hard' state the applied relief was cut round and details picked out with a special tool. Fine 'undercutting' is always an indication of good period or special work.

it may safely be assumed that many of these do not represent any specially prepared shade of coloured jasper. The unusual tone of colour is undoubtedly due to accidental variations in the local temperature or atmospheric conditions (actively oxidizing or reducing as the case might be) of certain parts of the oven in which these particular specimens happened to be fired.'

The period Wedgwood jasper colours remain: pale blue, dark blue, yellow, lilac, green, and black. All others are tone variations, experimental or accidental in origin.

1 There is a superb large tablet of *The Dancing Hours* in the Jordan Collection, Detroit, marked Wedgwood & Bentley.

2 When the colour is a ground jasper it is described as 'dip'; when the colour permeates the body, it is called 'solid body'. Many 'trial' pieces exist, many of them inscribed with formulae and instructions, indicating the ware's experimental history.

4. *Polishing*: a lapidary process the gems were put through after firing. Wedgwood writes: 'I understand that all our gems, before they are set, are put to the lap to be thinned.' A high-polished finish is often found on the edges of gems and medallions, and sometimes on the surface. It was also used on the inside of cups and rims of saucers in the fine translucent jasper ware.

For the collector, cameos, medallions, gems,[1] and tablets have the added interest of being specifically an achievement of the Wedgwood and Bentley partnership period. While there are infinite variations to be found in body and colour, the subjects in these classes are listed and described in the last Wedgwood and Bentley Catalogue of 1779. (See page 197.)

JASPER VASES

After the death of Bentley, the work on the production of jasper vases moved ahead quickly; great progress was made possible by the experimental production of the partnership period.

Wedgwood found vase subjects in great numbers in the cabinets and collections of his patrons (many of them members of Sir William Hamilton's Dilettanti Club). Of these subjects Wedgwood himself considered the *chef d'oeuvre* (until the Barberini) to be the well-known Homeric Vase which Flaxman modelled about 1776. The cameo subject of this vase, which Wedgwood called 'the Apotheosis of Homer', was later matched with a similar work called 'the Apotheosis of Virgil'. To these vases were subsequently added highly ornamental bases with gryphons at the corners. They were also mounted on drum bases, and were made in blue solid body, black dip, and, it is said, grey. The first copy of the Homeric Vase, Wedgwood presented to the British Museum where it is now on view.

Every kind of classical style is found in jasper vases, and there is little point in attempting to list the immense variety in size and shape (in every possible combination of jasper colours) put out before 1796. The period qualities of fine under-cutting, smoothness of surface, and perfect firing, are all well in evidence in both large and small vases of these years.

These items were made on a large scale, and quickly travelled to the influential centres of European taste. Wedgwood writes[2] of an early order:

'I have just now executed an order, by the direction of a merchant in Manchester, for an assortment of my jasper ornaments, with blue grounds & white figures,

[1] Used variously in the following applications:

Rings	Snuff boxes	Window shutters	Buckles	Hangers	Chests of Drawers
Chatelaines	Etui cases	Metal vases	Bracelets	Swords	Cabinets
Chains	Patch boxes	Metal urns	Brooches	Daggers	Watch keys
Scarf pins	Toilet boxes	Metal lamps	Door handles	Buffets	Lockets
Hair pins	Work boxes	Metal boxes	Bell-pull	Chairs	Coat buttons
Watches	Desks	Coach panels	handles	Opera glasses	Smelling bottles
			Cloak pins	Hat pins	Swivels, &c.

[2] To Sir William Hamilton.

PLATE III

Wedgwood and Wedgwood-Greatbatch coloured glazed wares. The teapoy is impress marked Wedgwood. The pineapple relief teapot carries the imitation Chinese seal mark and may be by Greatbatch. The pineapple teapot (front) is more typical of the partnership products. It should be noted that the handles in all cases have terminations, unlike handled items which bear the Wedgwood impress mark. The grape-relief is typical of the fruit style in decorative application

which he tells me are for the King of Naples. If so, you will perhaps see them in a short time, and I mention this to beg the favour of your correction if you think any of them worth so much of your notice. One thing I persuade myself you will observe, that they have been objects of very great labour & time, every ornament & leaf being first made in a separate mould, then laid upon the vase with great care & accuracy, and afterwards wrought over again upon the vase itself by an artist equal to the work; for from the beginning I determined to spare neither time nor expence in modelling & finishing my ornaments, and I have the satisfaction to find that my plan has hitherto met with the approbation of my friends, and that purchasers of every nation declare them to be the highest finished & cheapest ornaments now made in Europe. — I lamented much that I could not obtain liberty of the merchant to send a vase, the finest & most perfect I have ever made, and which I have since presented to the British Museum — It is 18 inches high. Mr. Chas Greville saw it, & wished it was in his Majesties cabinet at Naples.'

With his monumental achievement of the Portland Vase copies Wedgwood gained that 'approbation' for ever.

The full account of the Portland Vase copies, an adventure which celebrates the last few years of Wedgwood's life, and which produced the finest examples of his work in jasper, I have given in my monograph on that subject.[1] Here it is only necessary to note again the immense labour and expense Wedgwood undertook in the years 1786 to 1790 to make a perfect reproduction of what was considered by his age to be the greatest minor work of the entire Graeco-Roman period.

Today, we might be inclined to criticize as 'slavish' the typically eighteenth-century devotion to 'Nature' which Wedgwood exhibited in the venture of the Portland Copies. But the neo-Classical Age's prediliction was for 'Reason, Truth, and Nature', and we can only remark it. These were the criteria of his time, and Wedgwood observed them scrupulously. Whether or not such standards are absolute is for philosophers to argue; so far as the ceramics student is concerned, it is the quality of the work embodying the criteria which matters. In Wedgwood's imitative wares we find countless ceramic successes which have remained supreme in their sphere. Among them the Portland Vase copies are the perfect synthesis of Wedgwood's genius with the limitations of his age.

JASPER CANDLESTICKS, FIGURES, AND BUSTS

Candlestick and taperstick styles are rare in jasperware, but are more commonly found in basaltes. Such items, though their sconces might be fired separately, offered a much larger and heavier mass to the kiln, and the nature of jasper being 'whimsical', were far more difficult to produce.

Among the finest candlesticks in jasper are the rare solid pale blue and white Tritons. Modelled by Flaxman, the Tritons are also found in basaltes, usually

[1] *The Portland Vase and the Wedgwood Copies.* WOLF MANKOWITZ (Deutsch, 1952).

97

somewhat smaller in size and without comparable strength and detail. The lattice-work net on one of the illustrated figures anticipates the tri-coloured basket and dice work which was to be so beautiful a feature of coloured jasper.

Flaxman also designed two pairs of standing figures of Ceres and Cybele which were used in both jasper and basaltes as candlesticks. The finest examples are in pale blue solid body, the figures being solid white. Similar items were put out about 1800 in blue jasper dip, but without comparable undercutting, the dip very often 'bleeding' badly.

Flaxman also modelled a series of gods which were made in both waxen body and jasper, and were mounted on drum bases in blue and white. These figures are of the greatest rarity, and among the original set were the following:

Neptune, 2 feet high.

Triton, 2 feet high.

Polyphemus, 19 inches x 16 inches.

Morpheus, a reclining figure, 25 inches long.

Ceres, a sitting figure.

Ganymede, from the Florentine Museum, 12 inches.

Bacchus, after Sansovino, 11 inches.

Bacchus, after Michael Angelo, 11 inches.

Bacchus (another), $10\frac{3}{4}$ inches.

Faun, $10\frac{3}{4}$ inches.

Apollo, 11 inches.

Mercury, 11 inches.

Venus (Medici) $10\frac{1}{2}$ inches.

Venus, rising from the sea, upon a pedestal richly ornamented with figures, representing the Seasons, $6\frac{1}{2}$ inches.

Certain busts were made, when ordered, in white jasper or waxen body. In a letter dated 1778 Wedgwood informs Bentley that he is sending 'a head of Voltaire in white Jasper, upon a Basaltes pedestal Richly ornamented with the disconsolate muse, her Lyre unstrung at her feet & other suitable insignia, upon the death of so great a man.' The well-known bust of Mark Antony[1] in white body (also to be found as a medallion) is another example. Such white jasper busts are extremely rare. The basaltes body was more manageable in bulk, and black the popular colour for such items. Also rare are the charming representations of a child sleeping, in several styles and in all the jasper colours.

In 1860 a series of white stoneware portrait busts were made by Wedgwood's, after models by the sculptor Wyon; but there is little likelihood of these productions being mistaken for early examples. The early white body has all the finest jasper qualities, while the late stoneware is poorly modelled and of an undistinguished body.

JASPER PLANT-POTS AND BASKETS

A great deal of attention was paid by Wedgwood to the devising of pots suited to the growing of indoor plants. Many delightful forms were made in several colours, for growing bulb-flowers and grasses. Forms used include exquisite representations of the bulb-shape itself, hedgehogs, bee-hives, urns, and 'ruin'd columns'. Again these items are more common in basaltes. Superb flower and fruit baskets in 'strap' or 'basket' style were made, often in tri-colour jasper.

[1] Often wrongly described as 'Terror', the head of Antony was a pair with another of Cleopatra.

JASPER ANIMALS

Wedgwood felt the representation of animals to be out of taste, and few were made during his life, although pug dogs and elephants are catalogued and were probably made in both jasper and basaltes.

Mythical animals such as sphinxes and gryphons were made in jasper, both as decorative figures and as candlesticks and oil-lamps. Lions also were made in jasper as paper-weights and book-ends. Small animals in basaltes are all late productions, many of them being put out in the present century.

JASPER TEA-WARE

A large class of items for tea and chocolate use were made in fine jasper. The *cabaret à deux* was probably the largest single group in this class, comprising a tea or chocolate pot, a sugar-box, a cream jug, two cups and saucers and a tray. Complete tea services are unknown and would have been extremely expensive.

Jasper cups and saucers were made in large variety, both handled and otherwise, in all the jasper colours, and sometimes in three or more colours.

All the items in this group are distinguished by fine undercutting in their cameo decoration, as well as by excellent engine-turning, lapidary polishing, and perfection of body. The latter is so fine as to bring many items in this group closer to translucent porcelain than are many nineteenth-century bone chinas.

JASPER PORTRAITS

In the earliest class of jasper products, together with cameos, intaglios, and medallions, are superb portraits in all sizes, and with every colour of ground.

These portraits fall into two broad groups: Ancients, and Moderns. In the former group are included mythical subjects, Greek, Roman, and Egyptian kings. In the latter are famous statesmen, scientists, authors, artists, soldiers and sailors, many of them modelled from life. Others were modelled from famous portraits, or were bought from modellers like Tassie and reproduced in jasper and basaltes. The most interesting subjects from all points of view are those of Wedgwood's contemporaries who were modelled from life.

Wedgwood portraiture is of great importance in the history of iconography, representing as it does an early mechanical means of exact reproduction in quantity. So finely perfected was the technique in jasper, that the smallest cameo heads will be seen under the glass to possess the completest detail. In order to ensure the truth of his portraits to nature, Wedgwood used fine modellers, principally Hackwood, Flaxman and Joachim Smith. Unfortunately, because of his suppression of individual credits in the interests of his trade mark, relatively few subjects can be certainly attributed. (See page 197 *et seq.*, for list of portrait subjects).

CHAPTER FOUR

BLACK BASALTES
1767-1796

BLACK BASALTES
1767-1796

BLACK, so-called Egyptian ware, was a traditional Staffordshire product, common to the potters of the pre-Wedgwood period, the basic constituent, a black colouring, being freely available in the district. Simeon Shaw's account of blackware is concise:

> 'In the Egyptian Black Clay of the present day, a proportion of *Car* is introduced; it is an oxide of iron suspended in the water drained from the Coal Mines, and procured thus: Being of a specific gravity greater than that of water, it forms a sediment at the bottom of the channel of the stream that conveys it from the mine: when a considerable quantity is thus lodged in a certain space, the stream, to that extent, is diverted from its usual course; and the car is thrown out of the channel, from whence the water has been turned off, upon the adjoining banks; where it remains till dry. Sometimes small pits or ponds are made on the adjoining banks, and the car is scooped from the bottom of the channel, and thrown into them, without diverting the course of the water. When it is sufficiently dry, it is sold at the rate of one guinea per cart-load. Being very useful for Busts, &c. Mr. Josiah Wedgwood, prepared it of a superior quality in grain, and blacker in colour; and obtained a patent for its entire application. His numerous beautiful productions of this body remain unrivalled. But the patent was given up, in consequence of Mr. Palmer, of Hanley, satisfactorily proving, that the articles had been used some time before Mr. Wedgwood commenced business.'

In 'preparing it of a superior quality' Wedgwood used manganese to obtain a richer black, west-country clay to give a finer texture, and much greater care in the cleansing and preparing of the native 'car'. But these measures were not so simple to effect as they are to describe.

In developing the ware he eventually named 'Basaltes . . . a fine black porcelain bisque', Wedgwood undertook considerable experiment. Wedgwood basaltes is, in consequence, as different from traditional blackware, as is Wedgwood Queensware from the cream-body out of which it was developed. Though the name is today generally applied to blackwares from all makers,[1] basaltes properly speaking is Wedgwood only.

Wedgwood began his work on blackware in about 1767. He was concerned with developing it as a body for making vases and decorative wares to supplement the fine range of useful ware he had already achieved in cream colour. In that year he wrote to Bentley:

> 'I am picking up every design & improvement for a Vase work, & am every day more & more convinced that it will answer to our wishes. . . . I am preparing designs, Models, Moulds, Clays, Colours, &c. &c. for Vase work, by wch means we shall be able to do business effectually 12 months sooner than we could without these preparatory steps, & I have no fear but it will answer our utmost wishes. . . . Many of my experiments turn out to my wishes, & convince me more & more, of the extensive capability of our Manufacture for farther improvements.'

The earliest description of basaltes is contained in a letter dated August 1768, where Wedgwood describes it in terms of the original it was intended to imitate, 'Etruscan bronze':[2]

> ' . . . a basket containing 2 Etruscan bronze Vases full of my best compliments to Miss Tarleton, and beg her acceptance of them as an offering first fruits.'

This reference suggests very strongly that the basaltes body was not yet perfected. In which case it follows that Wedgwood was at Etruria and in partnership with Bentley before the period of basaltes begins. In fact, on 30th August 1768 Wedgwood wrote to Bentley to report progress in firing the new blackware:

> 'There are 3 other imperfect ones to show you a little into the light of our imperfections in the manufacturing of these delicate compositions. . . . Every Vase in the last Kiln were spoil'd. & that only by such a degree of variation in the fire as scarcely affected our cream colour bisket at all.'

By February 1769, Wedgwood was writing from London that he 'could sell 50 or 100 pounds worth per day' of ware; and he requests Bentley to put as many hands as possible on to production, that 'the great demand here may not be baulked'. Especially, Wedgwood requested, 'some large Black Vases' — from which it would appear that by now the partners had basaltes under control.

Perfect basaltes items, therefore, date from 1769, although interesting pieces issued by Wedgwood in an imperfect condition before this date certainly exist. The sale of 'seconds' has always been a feature of pottery production, and the Wedgwood factory has not — contrary to many idealistic accounts — differed in this. Without selling his seconds, Wedgwood's financial risks would have been too great to be borne, and Wedgwood fully understood that a perfectionist bankrupt could produce little pottery.

---

[1] Grant lists some fifty known impress marks on 'basaltes'.
[2] 'Etruscan' was Wedgwood's name for basaltes until it was transferred to encaustic decorated ware only.

In this connection the late Harry Barnard quotes[1] an interesting letter:

'I have settled a plan & method with Mr. Coward' (the famous wood carver who worked for the Brothers Adam, Architects of the Adelphi, London) 'to tinker all the black Vases that are crooked, we knock off the feet and fix wood ones, black'd, to them, those with tops, or snakes wants are to be supply^d in the same way. I wish you could send me a parc^l of these Invalids by Sundays Waggon, as he wishes to have w^t we can furnish him wth of each sort together.'

Mr. Coward must have made a very creditable job of the 'tinkering', because a month later Wedgwood writes:

'He has patched up some & bronzed others of the invalids, & sold them & serves the old creamcolour, & Gilt ones in the same way, & we have doctered, I won't say Tinkered, near £100 worth of what we deemed reprobates here, & by next weeks end I believe shall not have a single waster left. I have got an excellent cement, which we can even mould into ornaments, which grow nearly as hard as the ware & scarcely to be distinguish^d from it, with this we have done the Vases intended to be sold as seconds, & have converted them into best — In short we are arriv'd to such a degree of perfection in the Art of V: making & V: mending that we have not had two seconds in the three last ovenfulls, nor even a single one that I know of.'

These 'reprobate' but 'doctered' items are rare, but badly fire-cracked items in basaltes come to hand from time to time, repaired exceptionally well in some kind of bituminous body, the work well worth the study of contemporary repairers.

The styles which were immediately successful in the basaltes body, were the 'engine-turned'[2] fluted decoration, and relief decoration. The first time Wedgwood showed the London dilettanti his so-called Bedford Vase, its relief decoration was greatly admired:

'The Bassrelief upon the Medalion of the Bedford Vase is universaly admir'd wch I look upon as a propitious omen for that species of ornamenting, we have about a doz^n of them ord^d — all to be the very first that come. Mr. Cox has been running about with one (by desire) to several Noblemen this Even^g & says I must ord^r 1000, he says the Medallion alone wo^d sell it.'

The actual number of vase shapes issued by Wedgwood and Bentley in basaltes is not known, but Barnard computed that of the four hundred ornamental pieces[3] shown

---

[1] *Chats on Wedgwood Ware* (Fisher Unwin, 1924).

[2] An improved pottery turning-lathe was invented about 1764 by J. Baddeley of Eastwood near Hanley, and T. Greatbach, a turner in the employ of Palmer of Hanley. (Whether or not the improvements were stolen is neither here nor there). Wedgwood tried unsuccessfully (according to Shaw) to prevent the improved lathe being used by smaller potters by offering to pay twelve guineas each for them, if Baddeley would undertake to make that price general. The lathes were quickly installed in the Brick House Works, and improved through use, Wedgwood applying his customary energy to studying the new tool's possibilities. It was used extensively on redwares, but especially developed in relation to basaltes decoration. Engine turning was also applied by Wedgwood to his other wares, but throughout his life served as a principal method of decorating all classes of basaltes.

[3] These four hundred shapes were also issued in cream-colour, agate, marbled, pebbled, sprinkled, and later, jasper, as well as basaltes.

in the Shape Book, about two hundred and fifty are vase shapes, the remainder being ewers, lamps, tripods, candlesticks, plant-pots, pedestals, inkstands, and baskets. Among these decorative items, all of which appear in basaltes, are the superb Triton candlesticks and wine and water ewers designed by Flaxman. Variations among these shapes as such are small, although an infinite variety of relief and engine-turned decoration was used.

Basaltes was also the basis for another style of ware, the encaustic and enamel-painted 'Etruscan style'. This type of basaltes decoration was taken directly from the 'Etruscan' collections sold to the British Museum by Sir William Hamilton, and certainly in both colour and pattern, it often appears to be the best possible decoration for the black body.

Encaustic-decorated basaltes was produced in the complete shape range, much tea-ware being put out in the style, the black body being turned especially finely for the purpose. Certainly, with the exception of the table-wares which have an entirely individual quality, Wedgwood added nothing to the Etruscan style, being satisfied to copy the originals as closely as possible although occasionally it becomes more specifically a creation of the eighteenth century. But Etruscan ware remains, perhaps, the one style to which Wedgwood added less than was already there. The most that can be claimed for 'Etruscan' is that through it a larger section of the public was interested in the beauty of Graeco-Roman ceramic.

Wedgwood, however, thought so highly of the style that he used it for the six vases, 'the first fruits,'[1] thrown by him on the opening of the Etruria works on 13th June 1769; a fact which demonstrates clearly his humility and deference to the sources of his inspiration.

The total quantity of basaltes in every style put out by Wedgwood and Bentley, cannot be computed. Certainly it bulks the most important of the decorative wares, and Wedgwood's London office took large orders for it as soon as it became market-able. By early 1769 London was receiving 'fine cargos' of black medallions and intaglios. These smaller items were often sold in considerable quantity, by the set and cabinet, and are today still found in complete sets. The Kings and Queens, the Cæsars, the Popes and the subject intaglios put out at this time are well represented in most collections.[2] But according to Wedgwood, 'Large, very large Vases are all the cry', and such large vases were certainly made in considerable quantities. An order for February 1769 requests, '350 Dolphin Ewers, 445 of the Bedfordian Goat's Head Vases.' Wedgwood and Bentley basaltes had firmly established its market. It had become the 'universal passion'.

The range of basaltes parallels and extends beyond that of jasper, and the quantities put out far exceed the 'whimsical' ware. The same candlesticks, tapersticks, lamps, baskets, flower-pots, and vase shapes were issued in both bodies, the basaltes with

[1] 'The six Etruscan Vases, three handled sent to you a fortnight since were those we threw & turn'd the first at Etruria, and shod be finishd as high as you please, but not sold they being first fruits of Etruria.'
[2] See 1779 Catalogue for lists, page 197.

either a polished or a dull finish, being cheaper than jasper. But cheapness was not the principal appeal of the black body. It is a perfect medium for the display of shape and modelling, a magnificent body for the expression of the 'line of grace' which Michael Angelo recommended and Wedgwood followed. During the Wedgwood and Bentley period an astonishing range of vases was developed in basaltes. Their variety and beauty are well represented by the superb Grant Collection items illustrated in the plates.

Much attention was paid by Wedgwood to portraiture in basaltes, both in medallions and busts. Portrait medallions of ancients and moderns were issued, again parallel with the jasper range, details and undercutting being of the highest quality, while busts were made in all sizes. As Harry Barnard wrote:[1]

> 'There is not a finer example of the qualities of his black porcelain, or basaltes, than this; its highly vitreous nature when fired, and its capability of acquiring an excellent polish with age and ordinary handling and dusting make it a very real rival to bronze, for which it has often been mistaken at first glance. No detail of modelling or minute tool finishing was lost in the process of firing, and the extreme hardness of the material rendered it free from any wearing out or deterioration of surface either from constant rubbing or the action of damp or atmosphere, it preserved its original texture as when it left the oven, and even after being buried it quickly revives when the surface accumulation of dirt has been washed away.'

Certainly the basaltes busts of the Wedgwood and Bentley period are consummately modelled, and possess remarkable dignity. Contemporary subjects were taken from life by the best modellers of the day, while for models of ancient and dead celebrities Wedgwood selected the finest examples, so that first period heads are all of surprisingly vital quality.

Production of busts was first undertaken in 1770–1, the subjects all being antique. First models were obtained from a Mr. Oliver and were 'horrid dear', and useless to the mould-makers. 'If you could borrow some good bronze or marble busts', Wedgwood wrote to Bentley, 'for us to mold off wd be the best and cheapest way.' He suggested that, 'Ld Rockingham has many Busts wch he wd lend us at a word, so has our good frd Ld Besbro.' From these sources, then, the first models for busts came, and they were direct copies of the antique. In 1774 a number of models were bought from the model-making firm of Oliver and Hoskins, Mr. Oliver having been instructed by Wedgwood as to his exact requirements. The subjects were: Homer (large and small), Solon, Pindar, Plato, Epicurus, Zeno, Minerva, Venus, Palladio, Inigo Jones, Junius Brutus, Marcus Brutus, Agrippina, Seneca, Antinous, Faustina, Augustus Cæsar, Antonius Pius, Marcus Aurelius, Germanicus, and Cato. Hackwood was put on to their modelling, for so important did Wedgwood consider them that he removed his best modeller from all other work:

> 'We are going on with the Busts, but we proceed very slowly, it being a fort-

[1] *Chats on Wedgwood Ware.*

night's work to repair & mould one of these heads, & whilst this business continues we have no body to work at the Statues. . . . You will find our Busts much finer, & better finish'd than the Plaister ones we take them from — Hackwood bestows abot a week upon each head in restoring it to what we suppose it was when it came out of the hands of the Statuary. . . . The Busts will employ him for a year or two before our collection is tolerably complete, & I am much set upon having it so, being fully perswaded they will be a capital article with us, & Hackwood finishes them admirably. They are infinitely superior to the Plaister ones we take them from, as you will see more fully when you come to Etruria. I hope in time to send you a collection of the finest Heads in this World.'

This collection of 'the finest Heads in this World' ranged from the smaller items in basaltes to larger sizes in white body. But within the year Bentley received (as Wedgwood had promised) some larger basaltes heads, 'finished, & fired, & very good'.

Within the next few years, acting either to fill specific orders, or on their own initiative, Wedgwood and Bentley added to their full-size range of subjects, George III, King William, Henry IV of France, Homer and Shakespeare. Other antique subjects were put out, some of them uncertainly named by Wedgwood:

'We are at a loss about the Solon Bust order'd, having no other Solon than what we have called Demosthenes. He holds his head on one side something like the Roman Grinder, you know the Bust very well — Mr. Cox says it was called Solon when it first came here in Plaister, & continues under that name in our Catalogue — We shall send you one or two of these.'

The demand for the heads was very considerable. One order from Dublin alone requested over a hundred. By the end of 1778 the demand was so good that Wedgwood and Bentley could consider their range complete and concentrate upon producing the subjects listed in their Catalogue.[1]

Interest in basaltes heads suggested the development of figure subjects in the same body. One type of figure made in biscuit and in basaltes as well as white jasper is the 'half-figure', designed specifically for architectural use, and extremely rare. Half-busts were also made. But figure-making was not an enthusiasm of the partners, although they investigated the possibility. Wedgwood writes in 1769:

'I have not seen these sd black figures which have converted you again to a good Opinion of figure making, therefore if I shod waver a little you will not wonder. . . . My opinion is, that if we make more Vases than will be sold, or, find hands, who can make figures, & cannot work at Vases, then we shod set about figure making, but till one of these cases happen I cannot help thinking our hands are better imploy'd at Vases. If there was any such thing as getting one sober figure maker to

[1] See page 197.

108

bring up some Boys I shod like to ingage in that branch. Suppose you inqr at Bow, I despair of any at Derby.'

Several years later there is mention of two Muses 'model'd Statue size', an infant Hercules, and in smaller size, another Hercules, a Piping Faun, a Vestal, and Esculapius, as well as the jasper figures of gods already referred to. The range of animals already mentioned in jasper was also added to the basaltes production, but the standing figures of Voltaire, Rousseau and Priestley are known principally in the black body.

Certainly in his basaltes body Wedgwood possessed a decorative medium with a range as wide as that of creamware. Although useful wares were made in basaltes and with great success just as vases were made in creamware, the two bodies were intended by Wedgwood to complement one another. Certainly, in the Wedgwood and Bentley period, basaltes and creamware are the typical and representative productions.

DRY BODIES
1776-1810

PLATE IV

Wedgwood decorated creamware. The soup-plate (Chellis Collection) carries the Neville arms and is dated 1783. The jellymould is free-hand decorated probably at the Chelsea workshop. The teapot is lower case marked, and its spirited decoration unusually sophisticated for this style. In its cruder style attributable to local Staffordshire painters, this example is more likely to be a Chelsea artist's work

DRY BODIES
1776-1810

EARLY REDWARE

IT is certain that Wedgwood made unglazed red earthenware of the so-called Elers type, and it has been stated that he marked such items with an imitation Chinese seal mark often incorporating a letter W. Now such pieces would almost certainly belong to the first Ivy House period, during which time Wedgwood was satisfied to manufacture staple wares. In this period we know that he was concerned solely with turnout, and thought so little of his only new wares of the period, the fruit styles, that he left them unmarked. It seems, then, most unlikely that Wedgwood would have bothered at this time to devise a special mark for his redware, for it was, after all, common to most English potters of the period. It presented no great difficulty in its manufacture and could hardly justify the pride with which Wedgwood habitually impressed his name upon his later wares.

It further seems entirely out of character for Wedgwood to use a cipher style in marking. He was the first potter to thoroughly appreciate the uses of a trade mark; so thoroughly indeed that he made a point of restraining individual artists from signing their work. He believed that his wares were better promoted as *Wedgwood* marked clearly and distinctly, than by any other recommendation, cryptic or otherwise.

In considering the problem of Wedgwood's unmarked ware of the early period, I am led to disagree with the conclusions of most writers on the subject. Apart from the psychological factors referred to above, there are other objections to the suggestion that Wedgwood used the imitation Chinese seal mark. The evidence, in fact, for this assertion, is not at all conclusive. It is based partly on a W being some-times found incorporated in the Chinese seal; although this clearly *proves* nothing. The rest of the 'evidence' is built on the assumption that Wedgwood was the first Staffordshire potter to use engine-turned decoration.

But Wedgwood was only one to whom the improved lathe was made available by Baddeley of Eastwood, and we know that Wedgwood was never able to establish a sole interest in the tool.[1] Simeon Shaw asserts that Turner of Lane End, 'erected in

---

[1] His own lathe was built for him by Boulton.

the open ground before his manufactory, a machine by which he could turn his throwing engine and lathes': certainly Turner's engine-turned basaltes and cane-ware are of quite as high quality as Wedgwood's. The lathe was also available to Whieldon, for whom the manufacture of redware must have been of greater importance than it was to Wedgwood, and redware wasters have been found in considerable quantity in the course of excavating at Fenton Low.[1]

We know from the following letter that Wedgwood was working in 1764 on the improved lathe:

> 'I sh^d have wrote to you again though you are in my debt, but have been extreme busy on may acc^{ts} — have sent you a sample of one hobby horse (Engine turning) wch if Miss Oates will make use of she will do me honour — this branch hath cost me a great deal of time & thought & must cost me more, & am afraid some of my best friends will hardly escape. I have got an excellent book on the subject in French & Latin, have inclos'd one chapter wh^{ch} if you can get translated for me it will oblige me much and will thankfully pay any expence attend^s it. Tom Byerley is learning that Language, but I cannot wait his time. .. .. '

The first reference to the redwares being sold by Wedgwood is 'the first invoice extant' dated 9th February 1765 which Miss Meteyard mentions. We are therefore secure in attributing Wedgwood redware to the year 1765. But redware marked with an imitation Chinese seal was made before that date.

In the Schreiber Collection there is a redware teapot which celebrates the marriage of George III in 1761. This teapot has a crabstock handle and spout, and is decorated with stamped ornaments in relief, the centre subject either side being George and Charlotte seated and the initials 'GR'. This subject is flanked by reliefs of Chinese women with parrot and cage, and parrot and hoop; which reliefs are found on other red teapots bearing the imitation Chinese seal mark. It is reasonable, therefore, to attribute such seal-marked items to the same date and potter as the Schreiber teapot. This pre-dates Wedgwood's first redware invoice by four years. It very strongly suggests that the seal mark was used by some other potter(s), not so far identified; at all events, we are clearly not entitled to ascribe to Wedgwood redware items decorated with such stamped ornaments. It is not unlikely that the contemporary who used the seal mark continued manufacturing redware after the introduction of the improved lathe. He would not have been slow to apply engine-turned decoration to his ware, retaining the seal mark and giving Wedgwood further good reason for not using it; quite apart from the fact that by this date Wedgwood had his own impress in use.

[1] At this point it is as well to make it clear that the Fenton Low excavations cannot be considered conclusive evidence of the productions of the Whieldon-Wedgwood partnership. Obviously the same tips would have been used by Whieldon for discarded items in the years after the partnership ended. They are, therefore, a more reliable indication of Whieldon's production through 1760 to 1780, than of any work directly attributable to Wedgwood.

As one looks further into the ascription of the Chinese seal mark to Wedgwood, one finds less and less real evidence to support it. The first misleading reference to the use of the engine-lathe is contained in Arthur Young's *A Six Months Tour through the North of England*. Young made his tour in 1768, and he observed that 'Mr. Wedgwood was the first person who introduced this machine into a porcelain manufactory.' Clearly Young could not know the complex ramifications of the industry he was visiting, and his remark can only be taken to indicate that by 1768 Wedgwood was using the lathe on a considerable scale — as indeed we know he was, but for decorating basaltes, rather than redware.

Before leaving the question of the Chinese seal mark, one further possibility should be considered. The coloured glazed pineapple teapot illustrated on Plate III is typical of the modelling styles which William Greatbatch undertook for Wedgwood; it is, in effect, an excellent example of Wedgwood-Greatbatch, showing the green and yellow glazes of the one, on a typical style of the other. This item is the first coloured glaze example I have seen bearing an impressed Chinese seal mark; and it suggests the exciting possibility of the mark being that of William Greatbatch of Lane Delph, used by him until he joined the Wedgwood factory in 1788. This theory — for it is no more — may explain the baffling Chinese seal on some of the items which show the influence of Wedgwood but not his mark. Perhaps future discoveries will clarify the matter further, for although no further documentary evidence is likely to be forthcoming, the seal-marked pineapple teapot is probably not unique. Other marked examples may in the future provide clues to the still unsolved problem of the Chinese seal.

In attempting to ascribe Wedgwood redware of the Ivy House period, we must remain largely dependent upon similarity of shape to proven Wedgwood wares, although many stocks and handles are in styles common to both Wedgwood and Whieldon and provide little assistance. Redware indeed can only certainly be said to be the basic 'dry body' from which Wedgwood was later to develop several distinctively *Wedgwood* wares.

The most important of the dry bodies is black basaltes; so important indeed, that it must be given in any work on Wedgwood a section to itself. The other wares in this category are:

(a) *Rosso antico*: dark red to chocolate
(b) *Cane ware*: buff
(c) *Terra cotta*: light red
(d) *Drab ware*: olive grey
(e) *White stone ware*: pure white

These bodies were all made from local marls to which various 'ochreous earths' were added to produce colour. There are many variations of colour due to the quantity of admixture and the degree of firing; but the production of these wares involved no great hazards. Provided that conditions of manufacture were efficient, and the constituents prepared carefully, dry bodies were easily produceable.

They were inexpensive, and offered considerable variety, both in useful wares (largely tea-ware) and the decorative range. Almost every kind of utensil is found in one or other of the dry body colours, and highly decorative effects were obtained by the application of reliefs in second or third colours, after the jasper style. This last factor has often led to dry body items being wrongly described as 'jasper'.[1]

With experience there is not very much likelihood of them being so mistaken. The dry body is not as hard or as fine as jasper. Reliefs are hardly ever undercut, nor is the body found polished, although a fine lead glaze was necessarily used on the interiors of items intended to hold liquid.

ROSSO ANTICO

Wedgwood himself regarded redware as his manufacture for the cheaper market.

> 'My objection to it is the extreme vulgarity of red wares. If it had never been made in T'pots and the commonest wares, my objection wd not have existed. . . . I wish you to fix upon one of the *Bronze like* colours for heads for the cheap cabinets, as we shall never be able to make the *Rosso Antico*, otherwise than to put you in mind of a *red* Pot Teapot.'

But experience with the 'cheaper' body between 1776 and 1786, particularly when second colours had been used for relief decoration, brought it higher esteem than Wedgwood expected. On *rosso antico* (the new name with which Wedgwood dignified and promoted his redware) black especially was used to excellent effect. In this class the 'canopic' items decorated with the Egyptian symbols of sphinx, crocodile and lotus, stand out for the 'period' quality with which they embody the enthusiasm for Egyptian things which followed Nelson's victory of the Nile in 1798. Correspondingly, rosso antico is found as a relief decoration on basaltes. A desk set in the Vurpillat Collection decorated with children playing is of remarkable quality, and an early example of the style.

Rosso antico was used throughout the period of the second Josiah Wedgwood, but in items of these years a regrettable coarsening of texture is observable, together with a great loss of fine definition in the moulds used.

CANE-WARE

Cane-ware is certainly, next to basaltes, the finest of the Wedgwood dry bodies, and deserves good representation in any comprehensive collection.

The production of cane-ware during the first period was important, and a number of decorative styles were developed for it. It was made in decorative forms as plant and bulb pots, and in every kind of tea-ware, in all of which the 'bamboo' motif was popular; so much so that the description 'bamboo ware' is often used to describe cane-ware items in this style.

[1] A misnomer found even in WILLIAM BURTON's valuable book *Josiah Wedgwood & his Pottery*.

Together with the fashion for bamboo styles, came a resurrection of interest in the Prunus blossom theme, which was used in cane-ware, both as a pressed relief and as an *appliqué*, sometimes in a second colour.

Considerable decorative use was made of enamelling for which the dry light-toned ground of cane-ware was ideally suited. Many styles are found, but green, white and blue enamels are most usual.

In oven-ware, the so-called *pastry* style is found in many shapes. Cherry-pie, game, vegetable, artichoke, and others often decorated with fine lattice work to simulate pastry, were made and were highly popular.[1] Pastry-ware is a product of the period 1796–1805, but was resumed several times later.

The finest work in cane-ware is, however, the simpler relief decorated tea-ware (often lower-case marked). In this ware the finely ground body has an almost jasper smoothness; the potting has the ineffable quality of the best of Wedgwood.

TERRA-COTTA

The terra-cotta body proper is one used largely in the period of the second Wedgwood. Though it was made in sufficient quantity to merit a specific name, it is, in fact, another type of redware; but of a more orange hue than the rosso antico.

The most interesting examples of terra-cotta are those enamelled in colours with Chinese style decoration. This style of decoration was also used (to better advantage) on basaltes of the same period. Sometimes, however, examples (especially pot-pourri vases and tea-ware) have a great fineness, and the decorations of flowers, insects and birds are of great delicacy.

The finest specimens are of the period 1805 to 1810. When it was re-issued in the mid-nineteenth century, (and later again), much gilding was added to the style, which becomes florid and glassy with excess of enamel. Such later items are usually code-marked.

DRAB-WARE

Drab-ware is a development of the later period, and is found largely in shapes introduced by the second Wedgwood.

It is certainly the most successful original dry body style of these years. The olive-grey ground is frequently livened by relief in lavender, white, and brown, the acanthus leaf and other familiar motifs being commonly used.

The ware never won very great popularity, and fine pieces have a certain rarity. From the collector's point of view they exemplify very well the qualities of shape and style of the second Wedgwood period.

---

[1] 'The scarcity two years after Brummell's retirement, viz, in July 1800, was so great that the consumption of flour for pastry was prohibited in the Royal Household, rice being used instead; the distillers left off malting, hackney-coach fares were raised twenty-five per cent, and Wedgwood made dishes to represent pie-crust.' (*Life of George Brummell* by CAPT. JEFFS, 1844.)

WHITE-WARE

White-ware is a pure white biscuit of soft body, and is highly porous.

Though this soft white body was made during the life of the first Wedgwood, it is more important in the second period production. The special feature of white-ware is the beautiful lead-glazed interior, especially found in all sizes of the bouillon or chocolate cup.

White-ware (because it was frequently decorated with colour relief) is often wrongly described as white jasper; although a superficial examination of the body will reveal that its open texture is totally unlike the dense, practically pure, baryta jasper body.

White-ware glazed[1] was put out in considerable quantities during the second period. The glaze is a salt-glaze specially applied,[2] and is called 'smear-glaze'. Smear-glaze is typically decorated with jasper-style reliefs in blue or green. It is sometimes mistaken for salt-glazed stoneware by collectors who are not familiar with the manufacturing differences between the two styles.

Smear-glaze almost always reveals apparent brush marks when held against light; while salt-glaze proper will usually show the familiar pitting often likened to an orange skin.

* * *

Since there is a vast range of quality and taste to be found in dry wares, the collector must carefully pick and choose among them to find really fine examples. Such fine pieces certainly exist, and deserve representation, although there is no denying that, even at their very best, the later dry bodies are a poor successor to the wares developed and put out by the first Wedgwood.

[1] The other 'dry bodies', especially drab, are also found glazed in the 'smear-glaze' manner.
[2] See Glossary.

BONE CHINA
1812-1828

BONE CHINA
1812-1828

Because of the successes in earthenware manufacture of the first Josiah Wedg-wood, the firm's subsequent work in bone china under the directorship of the second Josiah, is often overlooked. But for the years between 1812 and 1828, the Wedgwood factory put out pure porcelain, much of it as fine as any the period can offer. It is difficult for a gifted son to follow a father of genius, and we know that the second Josiah had not a great desire initially to try to do so. But he will be remembered for his work on the Wedgwood bone china, for it was to the problems of its manufacture that he devoted his energies on returning to active directorship of the factory a few years after Byerley's management had reduced trade to a dangerously low level.

In 1810 Byerley, who was now looking after the London end of the business, wrote to the second Josiah:

'Mr. Mason of Lanedelph is in town & he called upon me, & in the course of conversation said that we should sell immense quantities of China here, if we had it — and that he should be very happy to make it for you — His china is, I believe, very good, & he has great orders for it — I only submit it for your consideration, whether you think it would answer, if Mr. Mason were to manufacture the china, & you were to have it enamelled at Etruria?'

But Byerley's suggestion was apparently not to the liking of Wedgwood, who must have felt himself and his factory perfectly able to make their own ware as well as decorate it.

In 1811 Byerley wrote again to stress the urgency of the need for a bone china ware to offer a market which, always capricious, now fashionably wanted to eat and drink from porcelain.

'Every day we are asked for China Tea Ware — our sales of it would be immense if we had any — Earthenware Teaware is quite out of fashion — & while we omit making china Teaware, we are, I fear, giving opportunities to other Manufacturers, which we should make better use of ourselves.'

During this time, however, Josiah was experimenting with the new ware. Bone china was a new experience to the Wedgwood factory, and there was no founder now to synchronize the processes of experiment with those of production and marketing. Josiah II had to find his own way. In a letter of 1811 he writes (somewhat uncertainly, one feels) that clay sent by Jonathan Lucas of Charlestown 'appears to be excellent, but the quantity sent is too small for a complete trial — I presume it would answer for china.'

By October of that year, however, experiments had carried the factory closer to production and Byerley writes:

'We are told you are making some china, & we are very anxious about it, as we are certain that we should sell prodigious quantities in Teaware, & indeed in every other kind of ware — I shall be very happy to hear whether there is any probability of our having any china to sell in 6 months.'

Since the production of china-ware was by now almost a practical proposition, Byerley set himself to investigate the demand for various classes of utensil. Obviously tea sets were the first and largest class. Byerley reported early in 1812:

'I believe you will want both the porringer shape & the common shape for cups when you make China. As soon as you have 6 to 12 Tea Sets complete, I would recommend you to send them, as we should sell them this Season, & we need not promise any that may be ordered in any limited time.'

By June 1812 casks of the new bone china, the first to be issued with the Wedgwood mark, arrived in London. An entirely new ware had been investigated, produced and put on to the market in some two years; a considerable credit to the talents of the second Josiah, and a reflection of the genius of his father.

Though Byerley has been much criticized for his lack of success after the death of the first Wedgwood, it is difficult to imagine any members of the original firm, used to the guiding hand and relentless will of its founder, being able to operate successfully without that sure direction. The uncertainty which one feels in the second Josiah, later reveals itself as a distinct lack of marketing experience. Instead of holding bone china in production so that stocks could be built up and the new range properly promoted in the busy end-of-year London season, he made the mistake of enthusiastically sending Byerley the ware as soon as he could — regardless of the fact that the summer was the worst possible selling period. Byerley wrote disconsolately reporting the poor success of bone china on its first appearance.

'We have sold one Set of China No. 599 — & a breakfast Set which is in the order Sheet but I do not expect to sell much till next Season — many families have left town — It will require to be known before our sale will be considerable — unfortunately the Sets were just a month too late here — however time is necessary to make it known.'

The ware won an immediate *succes d'estime* even if its marketing was not very intelligent. Byerley further reported that:

'Those who are judges approve of it very much. I think your china excels any English porcelain which I have seen — some pieces in which the glaze is fully run equal the French, with which I had an opportunity of comparing it.'

To consider how the first Josiah might have handled the new bone china is to see very clearly the limitations of the factory in the years which followed his death. He would, in the first place, have ensured that the ware was put into production on a scale large enough to serve the market he would have been quite confident of winning for it. He would have made certain that illustrious persons had his new creation in use, making presentations of it with proper ceremony to Royalty. Wedgwood well understood that fashion sways the market and that fashion, being created, is consequently controllable. He would have held the ware back until the public was properly acquainted with its merits, and then, when the demand for it was high, he would make certain that whoever could buy was served, and served while their desire was at its highest. The faculties the first Josiah had which make such enterprise possible, these were the qualities which the firm lost with his death, quite as much as his gifts as a potter. To any business the faculty for merchandising goods is quite as important as the ability to make them well.

However, in spite of the firm's uninspired direction, Wedgwood bone china found a market with the 1812–3 season. A large variety of pattern was demanded by this gayer market, this society of the Regency, as garish in its tastes as the preceding age had been restrained. The bone china is Wedgwood's *Regency* ware, and the patterns which decorate it reflect the taste we now describe as such.

The pattern range developed was considerable,[1] but the first important order was for a design which was already traditional and has held its place ever since. It was a blue-printed Chinese Landscape pattern of the Willow type similar to that illustrated on Figure 110. It was followed by another pattern described as 'Chinese flowers in red brown and colours, with gold edge'. This latter pattern proved popular and several colours were used; the style is illustrated on Figure 114. Floral motifs taken largely from Pillement's *Flowers* were also popular, the decorative treatment tending to be brighter than ever Wedgwood had put out before. Such botanical motifs were printed and enamelled over and lack fine detail. The shade, however, of the earlier taste served by the firm's founder asserted itself, and an embossed vine design executed by William Hackwood in 1812 found a good market.

The range of ware comprises tea-ware (prices for tea-sets were between three and four guineas), coffee-ware, fruit services, and smaller decorative items, such as inkwells, miniature baskets, and some small vases. Many of the shapes used were new ones and Wedgwood bone china is often, because of this and its style of decoration, mistaken for Swansea and other better-known contemporary manufactories of fine porcelain. Wedgwood bone china items are marked, however, usually in red uppercase mark, over the glaze (a fact which often results in the partial obliteration of the

---

[1] See list of bone china patterns on page 125.

mark). The mark is also found in blue — usually on blue printed wares — and in black, and gold.

The quality of Wedgwood bone china is extremely uneven, some of it being closer to the pearl-ware body, and very dense. Other examples, mostly the smaller decorative items, are of the finest quality, and often superior to the best productions of the traditional porcelain-producing factories of the period.

Collectors of Wedgwood have only in the past few years turned their attention to the firm's work in bone china; this being, in fact, the first note of any detail to have been published on the subject. Certainly the rarity of the ware will make it increasingly valuable, and further research is certain to produce new facts concerning its production.

The most important fact to have so far emerged in research is that of the extended period of manufacture of bone china. Orders have been discovered to reveal its production up to 1828. In 1820, stone china, a much denser and cruder body, came into manufacture, and this and the 'New Pearl Ware' began to displace the finer, bone china production.

BONE CHINA ARTISTS

Two artists who are known to have executed free-hand decoration on Wedgwood bone china are:

John Cutts of Pinxton, Derbyshire: His work was principally landscapes such as those on the tea-service in the Wedgwood Museum, and he was with the factory from 1813 until about 1816. By that year the demand for his style of work had dwindled. A memorandum from Winchester, dated November 1816, says:

> 'Cutt's Landscapes do not take, just now I am afraid I shall not sell any of his produce — perhaps fruit or flowers would do better, were they in his line. No. 701 teaset –4–4–0 I find is too high, if it could be reduced it might go off — they get all Landscapes up now, printed, and render them at 4/10 for 6 cups & Saucs not gilt — some are done very neat in purple colours and go off as well as the painted, with those that are not judges.'

Cutt's work, in effect, had become too expensive for the market, although relative to landscape painting on other porcelains of the period, it is not of the highest quality.

Aaron Steele: was with the Wedgwood factory in 1790, and by 1793 was being paid by the piece for his work. Many of the finest designs on bone china are by him, and he is listed as having worked Etruscan styles as well as bird subjects. The extremely rare examples of birds illustrated on Plate VII are probably by Steele. The pattern is not listed, and was almost certainly executed by the artist himself for a special order. There was, in addition to the above, an extremely fine fruit painter by whose hand

---

[1] Sometimes wrongly said in the past to have been 1805.

the ink-well illustrated on Plate III was decorated. Either this unknown painter or another of considerable merit,[1] was also engaged to paint flowers which, in conventional styles, decorate many early items of fine bone china.

BONE CHINA PATTERNS

The following patterns on bone china are described and numbered in the Pattern Book for the period:

512.	Chinese flowers, green ground, Gold edge & foot line & handles.
544.	Chinese flowers no ground, orange edge.
597.	Chinese, 4 compartments, & sprig in centre.
589.	China Tiger printed in red, shaded in red & gold edge.
590.	China pattern, gold edge.
591.	Butterfly pattern.
592.	Figures gold edge.
593.	Flowers & bird gold edge.
594.	ditto ditto with green printed ground.
595.	ditto ditto with yellow printed ground.
621.	Chinese Tigers printed on the glaze in black gold edge.
622.	ditto in green.
628.	Blue leaves under glaze, gold tracings on them and gold lines, Red flowers gold leaves to them & gold edge & line.
630.	Blue oak leaves under glaze, gold tracing, on them. Stem, acorns & tendrils & double lines gold.
646.	Blue painted Paris Sprigs with blue edge.
685.	China, small landscapes, gold edge.
693.	China embossed plain. } Hackwood 1812
694.	do. do. gold edge }
784.	New Chinese figures on China dessert ware TC pattern.
777.	Rose colour in bow border, gold edge on toy tea sett china.
776.	Dble purple Rosette border & gold leaves on china toy tea sette, gold lines & edge.
823.	Embossed Vine leaf gold edge, only one stroke down handle.
672.	China full border of flowers gold edge.
673.	do. with small groups of flowers, do.
674.	do. with larger do. do. do.
675.	do. Red Chinese Tigers, Red edge.
676.	do. Botanical Flowers, green edge.

[1] A floral painter named A. Cartledge is mentioned in the records, but the exact nature of his work is not indicated.

EMILE LESSORE
1858-1876

PLATE V

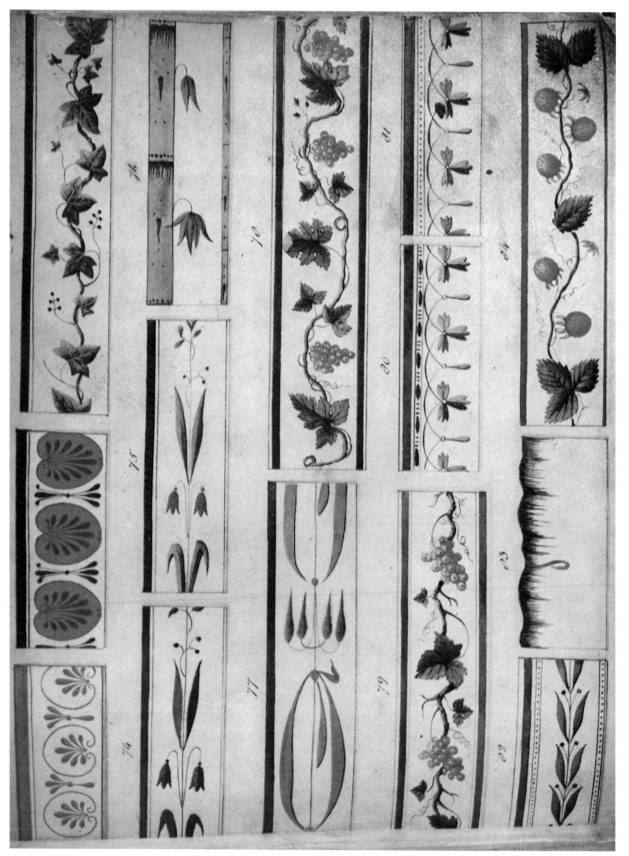

Page from First Pattern Book in the Wedgwood Museum showing typical border decorations for creamware

EMILE LESSORE
1858-1876

Out of the vast range of Victorian wares which stemmed from the Staffordshire factories throughout the period, very little commands the respect of the connoisseur whose eye is trained to the specific qualities of the preceding century. Certainly Victoriana is fashionable at the moment, but the fashion has been precipitated by a scarcity of earlier items; it has settled on us considerably sooner than it otherwise would. Undeniably there is fine craftsmanship to be found in the period, and its lavishness of gold and purple, its meticulous academicism encourage nostalgia. But although the collector is strongly subject to the nostalgic appeal, it is reasonably safe to say that most Victorian pottery will, when the fashion passes, pass with it into the limbo of the countless bric-à-brac shops from whence it was salvaged.

Of the specifically Victorian ceramic styles, however, two will certainly remain. The work associated with Louis Solon and the Minton factory, called *pâte-sur-pâte*, (a style which echoes Wedgwood jasper cameo work); and that which Emile Lessore executed on ceramic in the years 1858 until his death in 1876.

Lessore worked in the Potteries for five years, and except for a few months with Minton the whole period was spent at Wedgwood's Etruria factory. His health forced him to leave England in 1863, when he returned to Marlotte at Fontainebleau, but his work for Wedgwood continued on table-wares for several years more. In his last years he concentrated on ceramic tablets which Wedgwood's prepared and sent to him for painting.

Before considering the qualities of Lessore as a ceramic painter it is well to remember the problems of, as he himself put it, controlling 'colours of a stinted palette going through the fire.' The colours which can be fired are not comparable in range to those of the oil-palette, and the process of firing itself works changes which the oil painter cannot anticipate. Lessore, however, maintained that it was possible for ceramic colours to be 'rich enough to produce tints adequate, not only to compete with oil colours, but far surpassing them in brilliancy.' He experimented, therefore, as much in the technique of ceramic decoration, as in the exercise of painting, and concerned himself with developing new techniques as much as with painting fine pictures on a canvas which happened to be Wedgwood creamware.

The difficulties for the painter approaching ceramic were considerable enough for Stubbs. With all his experience of enamelling, his ceramic tablets still do not equal in quality his work in oils. For Lessore, who came to ceramic painting as a new art, the field was entirely unexplored. It was in no way comparable to that of over-glaze porcelain painting in which the painter is able to treat his medium as any other, and with small practice can exercise his art as well as his talents permit. As a painter Lessore was no original master hand. He was wedded indissolubly to the classic tradition, and most of his decorations on Wedgwood follow the styles of Boucher or Watteau, or point back to the Renaissance. But as an interpreter of earlier masters Lessore had a freedom and ease which loosened the academic bonds which typify many of the painters of his day. Although his subjects were conventional he was no mere fashionable painter mechanically following out a repertoire of set pieces. His line is free and his vision is simple, but fresh and authentic.

Lessore's work finds its best expression in tablets of all sizes, for he was always more concerned with the relation of his paint to the pottery body than he was with the immediate development of a decorative style for useful wares. Such a style he did develop, mostly in terms of costume pieces, domestic subjects, and children playing, but the freedom of his style is hardly ever at ease with the rounded surfaces of utensils — excellently simple in shape though they were. On the larger surfaces of the tablets, however, he was able to execute a large range of subjects, from a pastiche Last Supper,[1] to the spirited Spring, a Sketch for a Ceiling. The latter is dated 1873 and is one of the last pieces Lessore painted for Wedgwood's. In its delicate use of black and blue, combed together to produce a surprising effect of light and joy, the free and masterly sketch of Spring is certainly one of Lessore's finest works.

Lessore's limitations are most apparent in the vases he decorated, usually over yellow enamel grounds. In these creamware items — sometimes atrociously inset with jasper cameos — Lessore's admiration of Renaissance styles becomes a slavish copyism. When both he and the Wedgwood firm were attacked for this copyist dependence Lessore replied:

> 'Why? When they are the leaders in a trade; when they have selected all the classical and pure principles of fabrication; when all the more beautiful shapes of antiquity have been adopted by a manufactory, is it right to change these in order to meet the modern taste? God preserve them from such a change! It would be putting weeds where should be laurels! Is not Phidias always young after two thousand years? Who is the modern sculptor who has replaced him?'

An opinion as such with which one is not disposed to argue, although, it begs a larger question. For copyism is not at all objectionable when the original is experienced intensely and with perception, and the copyist combines with it his own

[1] In the Jordan Collection.

authentic experience. But if the copyist artist's inspiration slips he falls into pastiche of the worst kind; he supports his own flagging power with what he can borrow from the original, an unpardonable fault in art.

It is, however, a just and generally accepted rule that an artist be valued by the best of his work. By this principle Lessore is our principal pottery painter in the Victorian period. As to whether he may be considered a British artist in this connection, his own opinion was:

> 'Painters ordinarily change their national character before the works of the Masters, their models. Thus before Raffaelle they are Italians; before Rubens, Flemish, before Rembrandt, Dutch; specially devoted to pottery, I have become English at the Wedgwood's. There is my answer.'

There Lessore describes his influences and his affiliations. Certainly Wedgwood ware of the later nineteenth century is best represented by the pieces which are initialled or signed *E. Lessore*.

MARKS

Marks in the first period are not general, although uneven lower-case impressed marks are found on creamware items: the printer's type used is archaic and the effect distinctive thus:

wedgwood   **WEDGWOOD**

An archaic upper-case mark is also occasionally found, but the lower-case mark was more generally used.[1]

1764–1768
A neater impressed mark was used in both upper- and lower-case. It is found more evenly impressed, the type being of better design:

Wedgwood   WEDGWOOD

Occasionally experimental pieces in basaltes are inscribed WEDGWOOD.

1768–1780
The Wedgwood & Bentley marks (the '&' is always contracted) are as follows:

---

[1] The large variety of workmen's tool marks found on Wedgwood of all periods has never been systematized and cannot be used as an indication of date except in conjunction with an impressed mark.

The wafer and circular seal marks appear to have been used as convenience dictated, rather than in particular years of the partnership. The following in both upper and lower-case were used on both cameos and larger items throughout the period:

**WEDGWOOD
& BENTLEY**

**Wedgwood
& Bentley**

The following mark is found on seal intaglios, the number indicating the list number of the subject in the Wedgwood & Bentley Catalogue:

W. & B.

**Wedgwood
& Bentley
356**

The following mark is found on chocolate and white laminated seal intaglios, usually highly polished:

The so-called script mark exists so far as is known, only on one specimen — a pen tray — in the Wedgwood Museum. The Etruria mark, used in the earliest years of the new factory, is also rare.

Wedgwood & Bentley: Etruria

1785–1795

The normal upper-case mark, evenly impressed, regular in style, in all sizes, was used. By now the upper-case mark is typical, and is found even on the smallest gems and cameos; a fact which suggests that Wedgwood regarded it as the standard form for his trademark. Lower-case marks were also used in this period.

WEDGWOOD
WEDGWOOD

Wedgwood
Wedgwood

1790

The following mark was used for a very short time about 1790 (when the partnership was enlarged to include Byerley), but was quickly abandoned, although the firm remained Josiah Wedgwood, Sons & Byerley until June 1793.

WEDGWOOD & SONS

1805

The still unexplained mark which appears only on incense burners, and tripod stands, as follows:

JOSIAH WEDGWOOD
Feb. 2nd 1805

is certainly not an indication of the date on which the design of the items was registered — for the items were designed during the life of the first Josiah Wedgwood. Similarly the suggestion that the mark was used on pieces kilned during a new pyrometer test is unacceptable. In such a case items could have been marked much more simply, and less publicly. The mark occurs rarely, but at the same time far too frequently for it to be the mark of any kind of firing test. It is far more likely to celebrate the return of the second Josiah to the firm, after his several years away from the business following the death of his father.

1812–1828

On bone china the upper-case mark was used, usually over the glaze, in red, blue, gold and black:

WEDGWOOD

1859–1876

The important work of Lessore is always signed in full thus:

E. Lessore

32 Undecorated creamware confiture dish in the form of a melon. C.1775. Marked: Wedgwood

33 Cauliflower ware. The soup plate is a typical Wedgwood shape. The spout and handle of the teapot are more likely to have been made in Wedgwood's factory than the style illustrated in Colour Plate III. C.1765. Unmarked. *Diameter of plate: 9½".*

34 Creamware jelly moulds, enamelled in colour with fruit and flowers, and probably painted at the Chelsea Studio. *C.1775.* Marked: Wedgwood. *Height of mould on left: 8½".*

35 Creamware bowl and ewer with freehand decoration in coloured enamels of English birds, probably painted at the Chelsea Studio. *C.1775.* Both marked: Wedgwood. *Height of ewer: 11".*

36 Creamware gravies of the same shape, one decorated with 1st Pattern Book 'barley-ear' border in brown, both C.1780. Marked: Wedgwood.

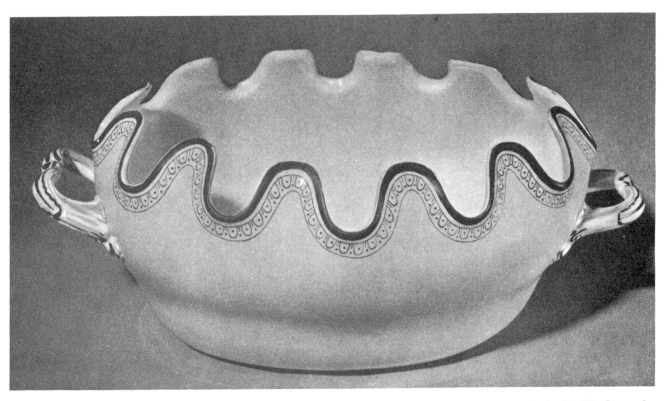

37 Creamware monteith with freehand border decoration in brown. C.1775. Marked: Wedgwood. *Length: 12½"*. Several shapes for monteiths are illustrated in the Creamware catalogues but such items are among the rarest in this body. Similar shapes were made in jasper.

38 Pearlware cress basket and dish, decorated with 'onion' pattern in blue enamel. C.1780. Marked lower-case Wedgwood. *Diameter of basket: 8½".*

39 Creamware cup and saucer with Liverpool Birds transfer decoration in purple by Sadler & Green on shell-edge style. C.1775. Marked: lower-case Wedgwood. The looped handle is noteworthy.

40   Dessert service 'Nautilus' shape, Queensware, consisting of one centre and stand, two sauce tureens and stands and nine compotiers.   Decorated with No. 384 design from pattern book of 1770.   Marked: Wedgwood. C.1798.

41   Dessert service, 'Nautilus' shape, Queensware, consisting of one centre and stand, two sauce tureens and stands and nine compotiers. Decorated with Number 384 design from Josiah Wedgwood's pattern book of 1770. Marked: Wedgwood. C.1798. *Centre diameter: 10".*

42 Creamware jug, free-hand decorated in colour, inscribed 'Success to the Lucy' and dated 1788. Marked: Wedgwood.
Height: 8¾".

43 Creamware muffin dish, decorated with 'Liverpool Birds' in black transfer. Marked, lower case: Wedgwood. *C.1775. Diameter: 8".*

44 Creamware glacier with border decoration in puce. Marked: Wedgwood. C.1790. *Height: 8".*

45 Pearlware glacier, decorated with green enamel and printed border. Marked: Wedgwood. C.1815, *Height: 8".*

46 Creamware teapot with Sadler & Green black transfer decoration. Marked: Wedgwood. C.1780

47 Creamware supper set with 1st Pattern Book border in brown and orange. Marked: Wedgwood. Fitted in contemporary tray. C.1780.

PLATE VI

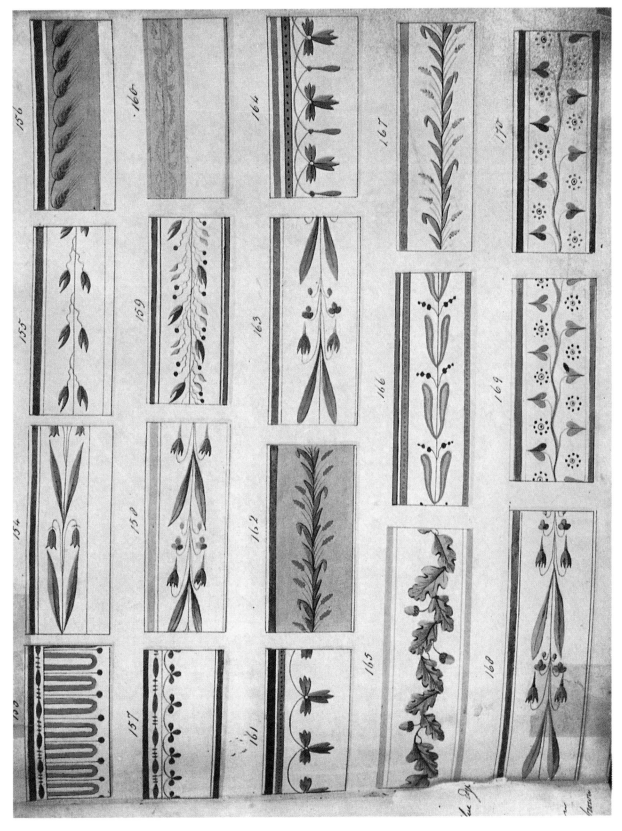

Page from First Pattern Book in the Wedgwood Museum showing typical border patterns for creamware

48   Pair of vases, surface marbling, thrown and turned, snake handles (1772), white jasper plinths, traces of leaf gilding, applied acanthus leaves.   Marked: Wedgwood & Bentley.   *Height: 14½".*

49 Vase and cover, in form of 'porphyry,' applied scroll handles and husk festoons, traces of gilding, No. 7 in Josiah Wedgwood's shape book of 1770.   Marked: Wedgwood & Bentley.   1772.   *Height: 14″*.

Vase and cover, in form of 'sprinkled porphyry,' pressed in imitation of fluted work. Black basalt plinth, traces of leaf gilding.   Marked: Wedgwood.   1783.   *Height: 9½″*.

Vase, surface marbling, thrown and turned, applied arabesque border, traces of leaf gilding, reversible cover, white jasper plinth. Marked: Wedgwood.   1783.   *Height: 16″*.

50   Garniture of three covered urns in brown and fawn surface agate with gilded handles and relief, and basaltes bases.   (Wedgwood and Bentley, unmarked).

51   Vase, in form of 'sprinkled porphyry,' snake-handles, black basaltes plinth, cream colour medallion applied portrait of Rafael. Marked, lower case: Wedgwood & Bentley. *Height: 8½″.*
Vase and cover in 'blue granite,' in same shape as (b) Fig. 49. Marked: Wedgwood. *C.1783.*

52   Garniture comprising reversible candlesticks and vase in surface agate, mounted on white stoneware bases. Marked, lower case: Wedgwood & Bentley. *C.1775.*

53 Pair of surface agate ewers with mask handles, spouts and relief in green glaze on basaltes bases. *Height: 7″*.
Marked, lower-case: Wedgwood & Bentley.

54   Pair of basaltes Triton candlesticks by Flaxman.   Marked: Wedgwood.   C.1775.   From the Tangye and
Grant collections.   *Height: 11″*.

55. Egyptian sphinx black basaltes. Marked: Wedgwood. C.1800. From the Grant Collection. *Height: 9½″.*

56 Ink stand, black basaltes, boat shaped, Canopic centre, applied ornamentation of scarab beetles, lotus flowers and other Egyptian motifs. Marked: Wedgwood. C.1806. *Length 12″.*

57 Wedgwood & Bentley wafer mark basaltes vase with relief decoration 'The Dancing Hours' by Hackwood after Flaxman. From the Grant Collection. *Height: $11\frac{1}{2}''$.*

58 Wedgwood & Bentley circular seal-mark basaltes vase, with relief 'Cupids and Wreathes' by Hackwood. From the Grant Collection. *Height: $10\frac{1}{4}''$.*

59 Encaustic decorated basaltes krater for pot-pourri or floral use. Marked: Wedgwood. *C.1775.* From the Grant Collection. *Diameter: 8".*

60 Wedgwood & Bentley lower-case mark basaltes mug with contemporary silver mounting, acorn and oakleaf relief. *Height: 5¾".*

61   Crocus pot, black basalt, pressed, glazed inside, decorated in red and white encaustic colours, applied 'Cupids and Wreath' decoration. Marked: Wedgwood. 1820. *Height: 5¾".*

62   Encaustic decorated basaltes cup and saucer, with freehand decoration and 1st Pattern Book border in red.   Unmarked, C.1770.   From the Grant Collection.

63 Basaltes snake-handled vase with heavy classical relief. Marked: Wedgwood. C.1780. From the Grant Collection. *Height: 14".*

64 Wedgwood & Bentley lower-case mark 'Fish tail' ewer, the lip modelled as a mask, and the handle terminating in a dolphin's head. Design from Jacques de Stella. From the Grant Collection. *Height: 11½".*

65 Wedgwood & Bentley circular seal mark basaltes vase with typical 'widow' finial to lid; Wedgwood & Bentley lower-case mark basaltes engine-turned ewer. Both from the Grant Collection. *Height of vase: 10¾"; height of ewer: 11"*

66 Wedgwood & Bentley wafer mark basaltes urn. From the Grant Collection. *Height: 13¾".*

67   Wedgwood & Bentley circular seal mark tripod incense burner.
From the Grant Collection.   *Height: 8″*.

68   Wine vase 'Sacred to Bacchus,' black basaltes, pressed, figure of Bacchus holding spout, applied goat head,
grape and wreath decoration.   Marked: Wedgwood & Bentley.   *Height: 16".*
Water vase 'Sacred to Neptune', black basaltes, pressed, figure of Neptune holding spout, applied dolphin head
and seaweed wreath.   Marked: Wedgwood & Bentley.   *Height: 16".*

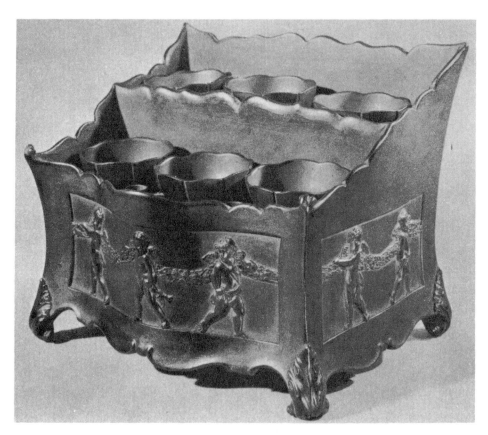

69 Wedgwood & Bentley double-tiered bulb holder in black basaltes, with
'Cupid and Wreath' relief.

70 Plaque 'Battle between Jupiter and Titan,' black basaltes, traces of bronzing. Marked: Wedgwood.
C.1768. *Diameter: 11″*. Plaque 'Feast of the Gods,' black basaltes, traces of bronzing. Marked:
Wedgwood. C.1768. *Diameter: 11″*.

71   Wedgwood & Bentley lower-case mark basaltes rum kettle with relief of Hackwood's
'Infants Playing';   contemporary silver mounted basaltes mug, lower-case Wedgwood mark.
C.1775.   Both from the Grant Collection.

72   Wedgwood & Bentley circular seal-mark basaltes vase, with
heavy relief ' Triumph of Bacchus.'   From the Grant Collection.

Height : 12″.

73 Basaltes 'Infants Sleeping.' Marked Wedgwood. C.1780. From the Grant Collection. *Length : 5½″.*

74 Pair of basaltes dolphin tripod-support incense burners, both impressed Wedgwood, one inscribed in encaustic: Josiah Wedgwood, Feby 2 1805. *Height: 5¼″.*

75   Candlesticks in the form of Triton in solid pale blue and white jasper.   Modelled by John Flaxman.
Marked: Wedgwood.   *C.1785.   Height: 12″.*

76 Pair of 'Rustic' candlesticks, 'Summer' and 'Winter,' modelled by William Hackwood, jasper, white on sage green. Marked: Wedgwood. 1784. *Height: 10″.*

77 Candlesticks, standing figures of Ceres and Cybele in solid pale blue and white jasper. Marked: Wedgwood. *C.1785. Height: 10½″.*

78   Snake-handled vase, solid pale blue jasper.   Marked: Wedgwood.   C.1785.
Height : 16".

79 Pair of solid pale blue ' dimpled ' jasper vases with relief decoration of ' Apollo and the Muses.'   Marked: Wedgwood.   *C.1785.   Height: 16".*

80   Early morning teaset, five pieces, teapot with cover, sugar box with cover, cream jug, cup and saucer and tray, 'Domestic Employment,' designed by Lady Templetown and modelled by William Hackwood in 1783, jasper, white on blue, thrown and turned.   Marked: Wedgwood.   1784.   *Height of teapot: 4".*

81   Teapot with cover, known as 'Brewster' shape, 'Domestic Employment,' designed by Lady Templetown and modelled by William Hackwood in 1783, white jasper, sage green dip, engine turned, leafage spout.   Marked: Wedgwood.   1786.   *Height: 5½".*

Cup, saucer and bowl, white jasper, sage green dip, thrown and engine turned, exceptionally translucent, reliefs by Lady Templetown and Diana Beauclerk, lapidary polished inside.   Marked: Wedgwood.   1785. *Height: 2½".*

82, 83 Cups and saucers in various styles of which six are shown in dark blue, pale blue, lavender and 'peach'. All marked: Wedgwood. C.1785.

84 Custard set of four cups with covers and tray, jasper, white on blue, thrown and turned, lapidary polished inside, applied acanthus leaf and scroll border, shell finial at handles. Marked: Wedgwood. 1784.
Tray diameter: 6½".

85 Coffee pot with cover, 'Domestic Employment,' design by Lady Templetown and modelled by William Hackwood in 1783, white jasper, blue dip, engine turned. Marked: Wedgwood. 1783. *Height: 8".*

86 Dark blue solid jasper bowl with engine-turned decoration and quatrefoil and banded ivy relief, the foot relieved with a band of white jasper, laminated and polished. C.1785. Marked: Wedgwood. *Diameter: 7½".* Formerly in Rathbone Collection.

87 Dark blue solid jasper flower pot with white jasper fitment; and an identical green jasper dip flower pot with fitment for growing bulb. Both C.1785. Marked: Wedgwood.

88 Bulb-pot, pale blue solid jasper, with movable fitments for growing living flowers in water. Unmarked. *C.1785. Height: 5½″; Length: 10″.*

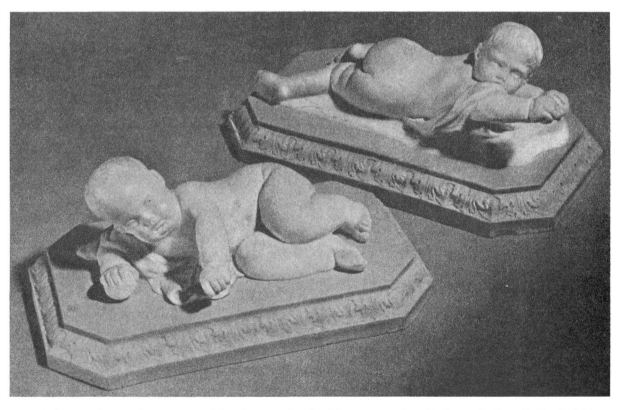

89 Infant reclining figures in solid white and pale blue jasper, by Hackwood after Della Robbia. Marked: Wedgwood. *C.1785. Length: 5½″.*

90 Cosmetics box in solid pale blue 'dimpled' jasper. Marked: Wedgwood. C.1785.
Height: 3¾"; Length: 6".

91 Bowl on foot, 'Bacchanalian Boys,' designed by Diana Beauclerk in 1783, jasper, white on blue, garland and grape applied decoration, lapidary polished inside. Marked: Wedgwood.
C.1785. Height: 7".

92　Oval and medallion ' Venus and Cupid ' attributed to William Hackwood, blue and white jasper in gilt frame.　Marked: Wedgwood & Bentley.　*Diameter: 5½".*

Plaque ' Choice of Hercules ' modelled by William Hackwood in 1777, blue and white jasper, ormolu frame with ribbon tie loop.　Marked: Wedgwood & Bentley.　*Diameter: 13".*

Oval medallion ' Erato ' attributed to William Hackwood, blue and white jasper in gilt frame.　Marked: Wedgwood & Bentley.　*Diameter: 5½".*

93 Pair of candle vases, dark blue jasper dip, decorated with 'Birth and Dipping of Achilles.' Formerly in the Allfrey Collection. *C.1785.* *Height: 10".*

94 Chatelaine or fob chain, set with two double jasper cameos, one—'Fortune' and 'Hope,' the other 'Bacchante' and 'Fortune,' mounted in chased cut steel, gentlemen's accoutrements attached including an eye glass, lock and key, seal, etc. 1786.
Length: 17".

Two medallions, 'Apollo' and 'Sacrifice Subjects,' jasper, white on blue, mounted in cut steel and attached to a satin band to form girdle. It was given by Josiah Wedgwood to Martha Merry, wife of Joseph Merry, brassfounder, Birmingham.

Marked: Wedgwood. 1786.
Height: 3½".

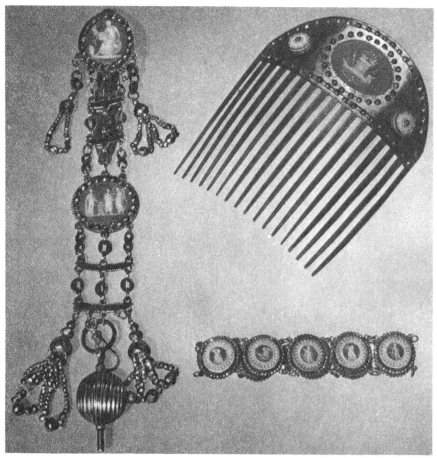

95 Chatelaine or fob chain with two blue and white jasper cameos, 'Sacrifice to Peace' and 'A Conquering Hero,' cut steel. Marked: Wedgwood. 1786. *Length: 8".*

Steel comb, with three blue and white jasper cameos mounted in cut steel. Marked: Wedgwood. 1786. *Length: 4".*

Bracelet, nine tri-colour jasper cameos, lilac, white and blue, applied 'Cupids,' mounted in cut steel. 1790. *Length: 6".*

96   Frame of twelve jasper medallions, mounted in cut steel by Matthew Boulton. white on blue.
C.1790.   Height: 16″.

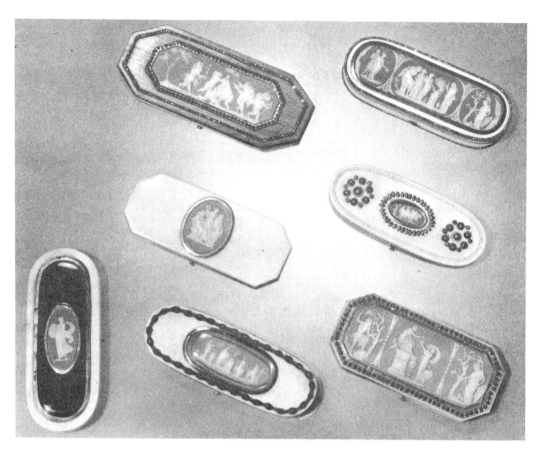

97   Ivory patch boxes inlaid with Wedgwood jasper cameos, all *C*.1785..

98   Perfume bottles in pale and dark blue jasper, all marked Wedgwood, *C*.1785.

99 Portraits on solid and jasper dip grounds of: (top, left to right) Marquis of Stafford, George III, James Athenian Stuart, Ralph Griffiths, (bottom) Madame Grignon, Boileau, Sully, Earl Cowper. Marked: Wedgwood, or Wedgwood & Bentley.   C.1775–85.

100   Wedgwood & Bentley medallions: (top, left to right) 'Marriage of Cupid and Psyche', 'Euterpe', 'Andromache weeping over the ashes of Hector', (bottom, left to right) 'Erato', 'Medusa', 'Sacrifice to Hymen'.

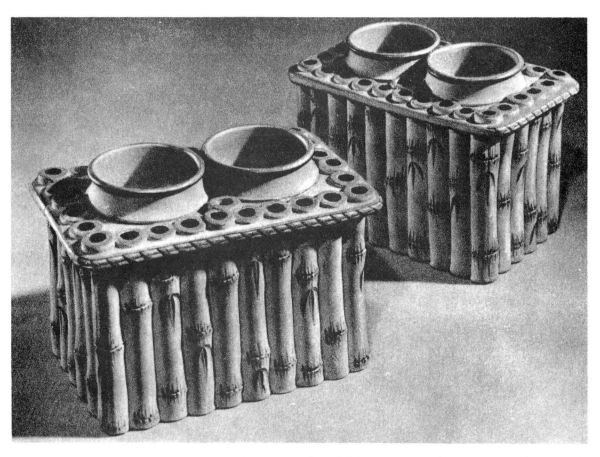

101　Pair of bulb pots, cane ware, handpainted with red, blue and green decoration, bamboo motif, glazed interior. Marked: Wedgwood. 1788. *Height: 5″.*

102　Early Morning Set, caneware, four pieces consisting of a teapot, sugar, cup and saucer and tray, painted in red and blue encaustic colours, bamboo motif. Marked: Wedgwood. 1792. *Teapot height: 4″.*

103   Caneware milk jug, acanthus relief in chocolate colour.
Marked: Wedgwood. 1810. *Height: 4″.*
Caneware ewer, chocolate relief. Marked: Wedgwood. 1790.
Height: 10½″.

104   Caneware dish, vine relief in chocolate. Miniature flower
basket, caneware with red relief. Both marked: Wedgwood.
Both C. 1790. *Diameter of dish: 8″. Length of flower basket: 4″.*

105   Dry white body vase and teapot with blue relief, glazed interior.   Both marked: Wedgwood.
Etruria 1810.   *Height of teapot: 3¾", vase: 5".*

106   Smearglazed stoneware jug with relief ' Bacchanalian Boys ' by Hackwood after Beauclerk, and
vine leaf on blue ground.   *Height: 6¼".*
Smearglazed lamp with blue relief ' Zodiac ' symbols.   *Height: 1".*
Both marked: Wedgwood.   1810.

107 Pastry-ware pie dishes. Both
marked: Wedgwood. C. 1796.
Length: 9¼″ and 11½″.

108 White dry body living flower
pot, blue diced pattern. Marked:
Wedgwood. C. 1800. *Height: 5″*

109   Bone china teaware, Chinese Dogs, green enamel on print.   Red-mark: Wedgwood.   C.1815.

110   Bone china teaware, printed in blue under-glaze transfer, Pagoda pattern.
Blue-mark: Wedgwood. C. 1815.

111 Bone china bud bowl and inkwell, painted over glaze with flowers and fruit.
Red-mark: Wedgwood. *C.* 1812.

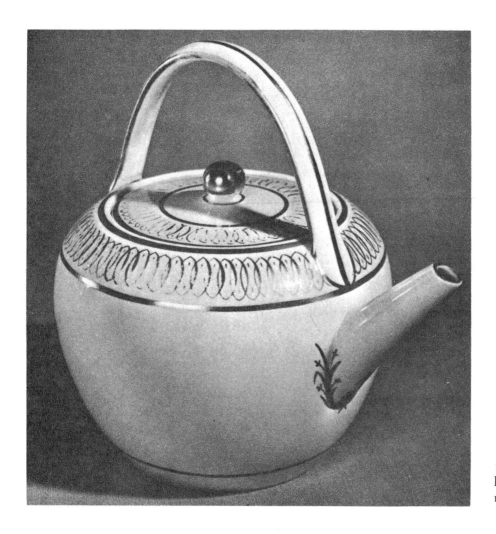

112 Bone china miniature rum
kettle, gold decoration. Red-
mark: Wedgwood. *C.* 1812.

113 Bone china plate and dish, Butterfly pattern, enamelled over print. Red-mark: Wedgwood. C. 1815. *Length of dish: 10″.*

114   Bone china teaware, decorated over glaze in gold, orange and brown.   Red-mark: Wedgwood.   C. 1815.

115　Creamware dish painted with mother and child by Emile Lessore. C. 1872.

116　Plaque (*size 4″ × 5″*) painted with boy and hens by Emile Lessore. C. 1872.
This plaque is unusual, being made of bone china the general production of which was
not revived by Wedgwood's until 1878.

GLOSSARY

GLOSSARY

AGATE. Pottery made to imitate agate stone by wedging tinted clays together so that the colours extend through the body. See *Variegated Wares*.

BALL CLAY. Dark-coloured clay, which becomes lighter in firing, quarried mainly in Dorset, England, but found in other parts of the world. Used to give plasticity and strength to the pottery body.

BAMBOO WARE. Dark shade of cane-ware made to imitate bamboo. Introduced by Wedgwood, 1770. See *Cane*.

BAS-RELIEF. See *Jasper*.

BISCUIT. Pottery or porcelain which has been fired once, but not glazed. Same as bisque.

BISQUE. See *Biscuit*.

BLACK BASALTES. Fine grained, unglazed, black stoneware, refinement of the earlier Egyptian black, made by staining the body. The various improvements made in the body by Wedgwood gave it a richer hue, finer grain and smoother surface.

BODY. Name given to the composite materials of which potter's clay is made. The term *body* is generally used when referring to earthenware or stoneware. The term *paste* is used almost exclusively when referring to porcelain or china.

BONE ASH. Calcined ox bones crushed and ground to a powder, and used as the main ingredient in bone china.

BONE CHINA. Soft paste body made from china stone and china clay with a large percentage of calcined bone added to give it whiteness and translucency. In 1812 bone china was manufactured by Wedgwood, but was discontinued in 1828. It was resumed in 1878.

BUFF WARE. See *Dry Bodies*.

CAMEO. Ornaments in relief as distinguished from intaglio. Specifically, that which is in one colour on a ground of a different colour. Used here to refer to those in jasper or other bodies made by Wedgwood.

CANE-WARE. Tan-coloured stoneware. In 1770 Wedgwood refined the clays used by peasant potters for their buff, brown wares into a new and lighter body which he called 'Cane'. See *Dry Bodies*, *Coloured Bodies*.

CAULIFLOWER WARE. Creamware modelled and coloured in imitation of a cauliflower, developed about 1760. See *Green Glaze*.

CHINA CLAY OR KAOLIN. Whitest clay known, found in England in Devon and Cornwall as well as other parts of the world, produced by the decomposition of granite rocks over a long period of time.

CHINA STONE. Known also as Cornish stone. Similar to china clay, but at an earlier stage of decomposition. When fired at a high temperature it becomes a hard opaque glass.

CLAY. A stiff viscous earth, found in many varieties near the surface of the ground or at various depths. It forms with water a tenacious paste, capable of being moulded into any shape. See *Body*.

COLOURED BODIES. Self-coloured body obtained by use of colouring oxides or ochreous earths. The early success of Wedgwood's dry cane-ware encouraged further research and the development of other coloured clays. These self-coloured bodies were, apart from bone china, the most important technical and artistic development by Wedgwood in the nineteenth century.

COMBED WARE. Pottery with a surface decoration produced by combing the wet, newly applied slip on the surface of pottery with a coarse comb or wire brush in a wavy or zigzag pattern. This form of decoration was developed in 1760 into its highest form by Josiah Wedgwood. See *Variegated Wares*.

CREAM-COLOUR WARE. Name by which Wedgwood's Queensware was first known before he became 'Potter to the Queen'. See *Queensware*.

DIPPING. See *Processes*.

DRAB BODIES. See *Dry Bodies*.

DRY BODIES. Non-porous stoneware body requiring no glaze. Made basically from local marls with additions of coloured oxides or ochreous earths to give the right hue. The dry bodies include basaltes, jasper, rosso antico, cane, buff, drab, chocolate and olive. They were made in a variety of shapes, both useful and ornamental, such as jugs, teapots, bough pots, vases, ink-stands, lamps, busts and portrait medallions.

DUSTING. Application of a glaze preparation in the form of powder to the surface of the body and afterwards melted in the kiln. See *Glaze*.

EARTHENWARE. Opaque ware which is porous after the first firing, and which must be glazed before it can be applied to domestic use.

EGYPTIAN BLACK. See *Basaltes*.

ENAMELLING. See *Processes*.

ENCAUSTIC DECORATION. Painting by means of a special palette of colours mixed with wax which is afterwards fused to the ware. It was done mainly in red and white on black basalt, by Josiah Wedgwood in imitation of the early Etruscan ware. See *Black Basaltes*, *Etruscan Ware*.

ENGINE TURNING LATHE. A lathe, equipped with an eccentric motion, built for Josiah Wedgwood by Matthew Boulton about 1763. By means of this lathe geometric, diced and fluted decoration were incised on vases and other such pieces.

ENGRAVING. See *Processes*.

ETRUSCAN WARE. Blackware with encaustic painting mainly in red and white. The name was derived from ancient Etruria.

FIRING. See *Processes*.

FLINT. Pure silica, the natural stone. It is calcined in kilns and ground to a fine powder. Flint imparts strength and solidity to the body and prevents warping.

GLAZES. Glassy preparations applied to the surface of biscuit ware to render it impervious to liquids.

Green Glaze. A glaze applied to shapes and decorations in various shades of green. About 1760 Josiah Wedgwood developed the green-glazed ware, to produce a new species of coloured ware to be fired along with the Variegated wares in the common glost oven. Green glaze was Experiment No. 7 in Josiah Wedgwood's 'Experiment Book' started in 1759. Since then green glaze, in many shapes, particularly wares made to resemble leaves, has been continually made.

Lead Glaze. Transparent glaze used on ceramics. It was first a powdered lead ore (smithum) which was applied to the surface by dusting and was called Galena Glaze. Later a fluid lead glaze, consisting of borax, china clay, whiting, etc, was developed and is now in common use.

Salt Glaze. Transparent hard glaze with pitted or orange peel surface, produced by throwing rock salt into the kiln from above, at the maximum degree of heat. When the salt volatilizes a chemical reaction takes place between the salt fumes and the silica in the clay, creating a thin coating on the surface of the ware. Thomas Wedgwood achieved a considerable reputation with salt glaze made at the Churchyard Works during Josiah's apprenticeship to him, 1744–9. Josiah's later improvements in cream-coloured ware, marked the decline of the use of salt glaze.

Smear Glaze. Semi-glaze or thin deposit on the surface of pottery, produced by smearing the inside of the sagger with the glazing preparation. This vaporizes in the heat of the kiln and settles on the surface of the enclosed ware. Smear glaze was a development following salt glaze and is often mistaken for it.

GLOST FIRE. Firing process through which ware passes to fuse the glaze.

GRANITE WARE. Earthenware with a graying or bluish mottled glaze, made by Wedgwood in imitation of granite. See *Pearlware, Variegated Wares*.

INTAGLIO. Sunken or incised design, the opposite of cameo. Wedgwood made a wide range of intaglios in black basaltes and jasper for rings and seals during the latter part of the eighteenth century.

JASPER. Dense white vitrified stoneware body of nearly the same properties as porcelain. When formed thin it is translucent. It has a fine unglazed surface. The body contains carbonate or sulphate of baryta. When coloured throughout the body it is called solid jasper. When the white body is dipped in a solution of coloured jasper it is called jasper dip or bas-relief.

JASPER DIP. Coloured solution applied to the white jasper body by dipping. See *Jasper*.

KAOLIN. See *China Clay*.

KILN. Intermittent or tunnel oven in which ware is fired. Intermittent or bottle kilns are fired by coal. The ware is placed in saggars to protect it from the flames and fumes during firing. In tunnel kilns, fired by oil, gas or electricity, the ware moves through continuously on trucks.

LATHE. Machine on which ware is held and rotated to produce an even surface.

LUSTRE. Iridescent or metallic film on the surface of ware obtained by the use of metallic oxides, gold, silver, copper, etc. Introduced by Wedgwood in 1805. The metallic oxides are suspended in an oily medium in which form it is painted on ware. To obtain a more complicated decoration than could be created by simple painting, the resist method of application was introduced. By this method intricate designs are painted or printed on ware with resist material such as china clay mixed with honey or syrup. The lustre is then applied over the entire piece and fired or fused to the ware. It will not adhere to the portion protected by the resist which retains the colour of the body. This type of decoration became popular in England in the early nineteenth century following the discovery of platinum. The metallic decoration of the eighteenth century, which has been termed silver and gold lustre, is not a true lustre process as known today since the metal was applied as a pigment with a brush.

MARBLED WARE. Earthenware made to imitate marble. The effect was obtained by laying on lines and splashes of different coloured slips which were sponged or combed together. *See Variegated Wares*.

MELON WARE. Ware modelled and coloured in imitation of a melon. Made by Whieldon, Wedgwood and other English potters in the latter part of the eighteenth century.

MORTAR WARE. Extremely hard vitreous stoneware body introduced by Wedgwood prior to 1789 for the making of mortars, pestles and chemical ware. It resists the strongest acids and corrosives and makes what are still considered to be the best mortars obtainable.

MUFFLE. Fireclay box or interior of a kiln to which flames have no access.

NAUTILUS WARE. Ware made to imitate the Nautilus shell. The first catalogue of Josiah Wedgwood's shapes compiled in the latter part of the eighteenth century illustrates the Nautilus shell dessert service composed of centre bowl. cream bowl and plates.

ORNAMENTAL WARES. Josiah Wedgwood divided his wares into two main classifications, ornamental and useful. Ornamental wares were further subdivided into the following 20 classes: 1. Intaglios and medallions or cameos; 2. Bas-reliefs, medallions, tablets, etc.; 3. Medallions, etc., of Kings, Queens and illustrious persons of Asia, Egypt and Greece (100); 4. Ancient Roman History subjects (60 medallions); 5. Heads of Illustrious Romans (40); 6. The 12 Cæsars and their Empresses; 7. Series of emperors, Nerva to Constantine the Great (52); 8. Heads of the popes (253); 9. Kings and Queens of England and France (100); 10. Heads of illustrious moderns (230); 11. Busts and statuettes of boys, animals and distinguished persons (142); 12. Lamps and candelabra; 13. Tea and coffee services; 14. Flower pots and root pots; 15. Ornamental vases in terra cotta; 16. Antique vases of black basaltes with relief ornaments; 17. Vases, tablets, etc., with encaustic painting; 18. Vases and tripods in Jasper; 19. Ink-stands, paint chests, eye cups, mortars; 20. Thermometers for measuring strong fire.

PEARLWARE. White earthenware body containing a greater percentage of flint and white clay than cream-coloured earthenware. A small amount of cobalt is added to the glaze for a still further whitening effect. Pearl was first made by Josiah Wedgwood in 1779.

PIE CRUST. Unglazed cane-ware made in imitation of pie crust in the early nineteenth century to substitute for pie crust in times of a flour shortage. See *Cane*.

PORCELAIN. Translucent vitrified ware which has been fired at a high temperature.

POT BANK. A works, pottery, factory or place where clay products are made.

POTTERY. Soft, lightly fired, opaque earthenware.

PROCESSES.

Casting. Process of forming shapes by pouring slip into dry plaster moulds which immediately absorb moisture from the slip. When a sufficient thickness of clay has adhered to the inside of the mould the remaining slip is poured out and the mould set to dry, after which the form is removed from the mould.

Notches in one part of the mould lock into the other ensuring a close fit. In drying, the clay piece contracts allowing removal from the mould. The cast article must be carefully cleaned and seams smoothed. Working moulds consist of two or more parts to facilitate removal of casting after drying.

Dipping. Process of glazing by submersion in a liquid glaze composition.

Enamelling. Pigments added over a glaze and given a separate firing in the decorating kiln.

Engraving. Cutting of designs on copper plate. See *Printing*.

Firing. Process of transforming clay into pottery by burning it in a special oven or kiln.

Glazing. Application of the glaze to the ware. This is done by dipping or spraying. See *Glaze*.

Modelling. Process of making the original pattern or design from which the master mould is made. From a drawn design the original clay model is produced with great accuracy and skill. Allowances must be made for shrinkage from 'wet clay' to 'dry clay' size and again during firing process.

Mould Making. Making of moulds so that many reproductions may be made from the modeller's pattern. The block mould is made from the original clay model. A case mould is made from the block mould, and from the case mould the potter's working mould is made from which the cast piece is produced. The working moulds are reproduced from the case mould as required.

Ornamenting. Process of applying relief decoration to ware while still in the plastic state. Clay is pressed into ornamenting or 'pitcher' moulds forming figures, leaves, scrolls, bands and other types of relief decoration. The relief is lifted out and applied to the ware after moistening the surface of the ware with water. The ornament is fixed by the skilful pressure of the craftsman's fingers. This method of hand-ornamenting has not altered since the days of Josiah Wedgwood. Embossed or hand-applied clay bas-reliefs, are made in 'pitcher' moulds by a figure maker and applied by an ornamenter, after wetting the surface. The ornament is fixed by skilful pressure of the craftsman's finger; and a sensitive touch is necessary to preserve the fine detail of the applied ornament.

Overglaze Decoration. Painting or printing patterns on the glazed surface.

Printing. Art of transferring engraved patterns to the surface of ware by means of tissue paper and prepared ink. Printing on pottery was invented by Sadler & Green of Liverpool 1755. Josiah Wedgwood bought the right to do his own printing in 1763. Printing was done in the Chelsea Studios in 1770. Wedgwood employed his own engravers to make his designs in 1780.

Throwing. Process of making ware on the potter's wheel. The name comes from the action of throwing a ball of soft clay down upon the revolving wheel. The ball is then centred on the wheel and worked up with the hands.

Turning. Process of shaping on a horizontal lathe similar to that used in the turning of wood. The 'Turner' receives the ware in its 'greenhard' state, places it on a 'chum' (a hollow drum which holds the piece) and shaves or turns the piece to impart lightness and finish.

Underglaze Decoration. Painting or printing patterns on the fired biscuit before it is glazed.

QUEENSWARE. Earthenware of an ivory or cream colour developed by Josiah Wedgwood.

REDWARE. Hard fine stoneware. See *Rosso antico*.

RESIST. See *Lustre*.

ROSSO ANTICO. Name given by Josiah Wedgwood to his redware, which was a refinement of the earlier redware introduced by the Elers brothers.

SAGGARS. Fireclay boxes in which pottery is packed in a kiln to protect it from the direct action of the flames.

SALT GLAZE. See *Glaze*.

SILVER LUSTRE. See *Lustre*.

SLIP. Potter's clay in a liquid state of about the same consistency as cream, used for slip decoration or casting.

SLIP DECORATION. Process of decorating pottery by applying slip over the surface in dots and lines or tracing designs with slip applied through a quill. Similar to ornamenting a cake with icing.

SMEAR GLAZE. See *Glaze*.

SPECKLED WARE. See *Variegated Wares*.

SPRIGGED WARE. Moulded relief decoration applied or sprigged directly to the body from a mould.

SPRINKLED WARE. See *Variegated Ware*.

STONEWARE. Opaque, vitrified, hard body fired at a high temperature, so named because of its excessive hardness which renders it practically impervious to water without glazing. Stoneware was the principal article of manufacture at the beginning of Josiah Wedgwood's partnership with Whieldon in 1754. Thomas Wedgwood was making stoneware as early as 1710. It is the connecting link between earthenware and porcelain.

TORTOISE-SHELL WARE. Earthenware made to imitate the shell of a tortoise. Metallic oxides were dusted on the surface of ware; manganese to give bronze and purple, copper for green, etc. When fired the mingling of colours produced markings in variegated colours. Agate wares are coloured throughout the body, while tortoise-shell colour is in the glaze only. See *Variegated Wares*.

USEFUL WARES. Josiah Wedgwood divided his wares into two main classifications, useful and ornamental. Useful wares are those to be used in the service of food as contrasted with those of a purely ornamental character.

VARIEGATED WARES. Earthenwares made by the use of different coloured clays extending throughout the body as in agate ware or by the mixture of colours in the slip glazes as in mottled, sprinkled, freckled, marbled and tortoise-shell wares.

VITREOUS BODY. A body converted to a glass-like substance by fusion at high temperature.

A TRANSCRIPT
OF THE 1779
WEDGWOOD & BENTLEY
CATALOGUE

A TRANSCRIPT OF THE
1779 WEDGWOOD & BENTLEY
CATALOGUE

THE Progress of the Arts, at all Times, and in every Country, chiefly depends upon the Encouragement they receive from those, who by their Rank and Affluence are Legislators in Taste; and who alone are capable of bestowing Rewards upon the Labours of Industry and Exertions of Genius. It is their influence that forms the Character of every age; they can turn the Current of human Pursuits at their Pleasure; and either be surrounded with Beauty or Deformity, with Barbarians or Men.

Great Improvements cannot be made without powerful Patronage; no Art ever was, or can be carried to great Perfection with feeble Efforts, or at a *small Expence*; and it depends upon the Views and Liberality of those who are possessed of Riches and Power, whether Individuals shall be ruined or rewarded for their Ingenuity.

It is to the Goodness, and generous Protection of our *most gracious* SOVEREIGNS, and of the *Nobility* and *Connoisseurs* of this Kingdom, that we are indebted for the Existence of our Manufactory: And it is through the Continuation of their support, and the liberal Encouragement of many *Princes* and *illustrious Persons* on the Continent, that we have been enabled to risque the Expence of continual Improvements; and to produce a considerable Variety of Ornaments; the Merit of which we humbly submit to the Judgement of those who are skilled in these Subjects.

The Variety of new Articles, which many of our respectable Friends have not seen, and Multitudes of Persons of Curiosity and Taste in the Works of Art have never heard of, render some Account or Catalogue of them necessary; but many of the Articles, and especially the Vases, being of such a Nature, as not to admit of satisfactory and clear Descriptions, several Parts of this Catalogue can only give a slight and general Enumeration of the *Classes*, without descending to Particulars.

We shall, however, hope to make the general Enumeration sufficiently intelligible; and descend to Particulars, where the Nature of the Subjects admits of it.

To give an Idea of the *Nature* and *Variety* of the Productions of our Ornamental Works, it will be necessary to point out and describe the various *Compositions*, of which the Forms, &c. are made; and to distinguish and arrange the several Productions in suitable *Classes*.

The *Compositions*, or Bodies of which the ornamental Pieces are made, may be divided into the following Branches:

I. A Composition of *Terra Cotta*; resembling Porphyry, Jasper, and other beautiful Stones, of the Vitrescent, or Crystaline Class.

II. A fine *Black Porecelaine*, having nearly the same Properties as the *Basaltes*; resisting the Attacks of Acids; being a Touchstone to Copper, Silver and Gold; admitting of a good Polish, and capable of bearing to be made red hot in a furnace, frequently without Damage.

III. A white waxen Biscuit Ware, or *Terra Cotta*; capable of bearing the same Heat as the *Basaltes*.

IV. A fine white artificial *Jasper*, of exquisite Beauty and Delicacy; proper for Cameos, Portraits, and Bas-reliefs.

The *Productions* of this Manufactory, may be divided into the following *Classes*.

CLASS I

CAMEOS AND INTAGLIOS

These are exactly taken from the finest antique Gems. The *Cameos* are fit for Rings, Buttons, Lockets and Bracelets; and especially for inlaying in fine Cabinets, Writing-Tables, Bookcases, &c. of which they form the most beautiful Enrichment, at a moderate Expence; the Price of the Cameos, with *several Figures*, being *ten Times less* than any other durable Imitations that have ever been made in Europe; and the Figures are much sharper than in those that are made of Glass.

The Ladies may display their Taste a thousand Ways, in the Application of these Cameos; and thus lead Artists to a better Stile in ornamenting their Works.

There are Specimens of this Kind already, that do no less Honour to the Heart, than to the Taste of the noble Lady, who chose this delicate Way of patronizing and supporting an infant Art; — which can only exist and be improved by the Aid of such generous Protection.

The Intaglios in artificial *Basaltes*, are most excellent Seals; being exact Impressions from the finest Gems; and therefore much truer than any engraved Copies can be; with the singular Advantage of being little inferior in Hardness to the Gems themselves.

In this Composition *Cameos* may be converted into Seals; without losing the Drawing, the Spirit, and Delicacy of the original Work; so that Gentlemen may have a great Variety of Seals at a small Expence; or have an Opportunity of making Collections of perfect and durable Copies of the choicest Gems.

By the Favour of the Nobility, &c. who are in Possession of original Gems, or fine

Impressions of those in foreign Collections, we have been enabled to make our List pretty numerous; but as, by the same Means, it is perpetually increasing, our Collection does not admit of a very methodical Arrangement, though the Numbers in the first Section of this Class, refer to an arranged Catalogue; and those that do not belong to it are thrown into an Appendix. But as our List of Intaglios is considerably enlarged since the First Edition of this Catalogue, and the Demand for them greatly encreased, by the Experience of their Excellence, we apprehend it will be proper to divide this Class into *two Sections*, the first containing the *Cameos*, and the Second the *Intaglios* that have already been made.[1]

SECTION I

CAMEOS

These Cameos are either made in a fine *Waxen Biscuit*, of extreme Hardness, with Grounds enameled of different Colours; or in the *artificial Jasper*, with blue or brown Grounds, the Colours of which penetrate through the whole Mass, like those of a natural Cameo, and admit of the same Polish: Or they may be had in the white waxen Biscuit, or in blue Jasper, at a very moderate Price, for those who wish to form mythological Cabinets.

EGYPTIAN HISTORY

1 Osiris, adored by the Egyptians under the figure of an Ox, named Apis, with Harpocrates upon the sacred Bark of the Nile.

3 Isis, wife of Osiris, with the flower Lotus.

4 Isis, the wife of Osiris.

5 The same.

7 Isis, with the Cistrum.

13 The Temple of Isis.

17 Harpocrates with the fruit and leaves of Persea upon his head.

19 Harpocrates standing upon the Bark of Papyrus.

36 The flower Lotus, or the fruit and leaves of the tree Penia.

42 An Egyptian Sphynx, with an Ape.

[1] Wedgwood used the work of the following artists, not all of which can, however, be definitely attributed.

Angelini.	Gosset, Isaac; 1713-97.	Parker, Theodore.
Astle, Thomas; 1735-1803.	Gosset, Matthew; 1683-1744.	Pingo, T.
Bacon, John; 1740-99.	Grant, B. and Hoskins, James.	Reynolds, Sir Joshua, P.R.A.; 1723-92.
Barret, George, R.A.; 1732-84.	Greatbatch, William.	Roubiliac, L. F.; 1695-1762.
Beauclerk, Lady Diana; 1734–1808.	Hackwood, William.	Smith, Joachim.
Burch, Edward.	Landre, Mrs.	Steel, Aaron.
Coward, John.	Le Brun, C.; 1619-90.	Stothard, Thomas, R.A.; 1755-1834.
Dalmazzoni, Angelo.	Lochée, John-Charles.	Stubbs, George, R.A.; 1724-1806.
Dassier, John; 1676-1763.	Mangiarotti.	Tassie, James; 1735-99.
Davaere, John.	Manzolini.	Tebo.
Flaxman, John, R.A.; 1755-1826.	Nini, Jean-Baptiste; 1716-86.	Templeton, Lady.
Fratoddi.	Pacetti.	Webber, Henry.

47 Saturn, son of Heaven and the Earth, holding a Scythe, and with an open Book at his feet.

52 The Coribantes striking their bucklers, to prevent the cries of Jupiter from being heard by Saturn, when Cybele had given the child to be nursed by the goat Amalthea.

53 The Goddess, Cybele, wife of Saturn.

55 The Goddess Cybele.

59 Jupiter with all his Attributes.

64 Jupiter.

65 Jupiter Olympus.

66 Jupiter with the Diadem.

74 Jupiter Olympus, sitting in the middle of the Zodiac, with Mercury, Minerva and Neptune.

83 Jupiter Conservator.

87 Jupiter sitting upon his Chariot, drawn by four horses, thundering upon the Giants.

94 Juno.

99 Jupiter caressing Leda, in the form of a Swan.

101 The same.

102 Jupiter transformed into a Bull.

108 Argus guarding Iö transformed into a Cow.

110 The Council of the Gods.

112 Janus with two faces.

115 Minerva born of the brain of Jupiter.

117 Minerva carrying the Aegis.

119 Minerva with the Aegis.

120 The same.

125 Minerva standing, armed.

128 The same.

133 A Talisman.

134 Mercury, son of Jupiter and Maia.

140 The same.

141 Mercury, the secret messenger of the Gods.

142 Mercury, carrying a letter, as a messenger.

147 Mercury standing, holding Aries' head.

149 Mercury sitting upon Aries.

152 Mercury, God of Travellers.

154 Mercury keeping the Flock of Admetus.

164 Hermaphroditus.

167 The three Graces.

168 The same.

169 The same.

171 Peace.

172 The same.

176 Neptune standing with his Trident.

178 Neptune upon his Chariot, drawn by four Sea-horses.

179 Neptune sitting upon a Dolphin.

185 Nereus and Doris, sea-gods, sons of Ocean and Thetis.

186 The same.

188 Nereide, a sea-nymph, daughter of Nereus and Doris.

191 The same.

197 A River.

201 Ceres, daughter of Saturn and Ops, Goddess of Agriculture.

212 The Goddess Flora.

213 The Goddess Pomona.

214 The same.

219 Night shedding Poppies, or Ceres and Triptolemus.

221 Apollo, son of Jupiter and Latona.

222 Apollo ditto.

227 Apollo with the Lyre.

232 Apollo standing.

234 Chyron, the Centaur, instructing Apollo.

| 804 | Ptolomy Philopater VI, King of Egypt. | 813 | Ptolomy Junior XIII, King of Egypt. |

804 Ptolomy Philopater VI, King of Egypt.
805 Ptolomy Evergetes VII, King of Egypt.

813 Ptolomy Junior XIII, King of Egypt.

FABULOUS AGE OF THE GREEKS

818 Prometheus forming a head.
823 Belerophon taming Pegasus.
829 A Chymera.
832 Media rejuvenating the father of Jason.
845 Theseus.
847 Theseus.
850 Theseus.
854 A Centaur carrying the branch of a tree upon his shoulder, and a Cornucopia.
861 Leander.

866 Cressontus, Timeno, and Euristhonus, drawing lots for the cities of Messina, Argos and Sparta.
871 Perseus.
873 The same.
874 The same.
876 The same.
877 The same.
878 Medusa.
884 Meleager.
887 The same.
893 Daedalus.

THE WAR OF TROY

912 Priam King of Troy.
914 Paris, son of Priam.
921 Hector and Andromache.
927 Achilles, son of Peleus.
928 The infant Achilles carried by Chiron a Centaur.
929 Chiron, Centaur, instructing young Achilles.
930 Chiron.
939 Ajax and Teucer.
940 Ajax carrying the body of Patroclus.
943 A Greek Soldier bringing the news of the death of Patroclus to Achilles.

947 Hector drawn by Horses.
948 Priam begging the body of Hector from Achilles.
954 Ajax carrying upon his shoulders the body of Achilles.
957 Diomede, son of Tydeus.
960 The same.
961 The same.
963 Diomede prevented by Apollo from pursuing Eneas.
976 Laocoon, son of Priam and high-priest of Apollo.

ROMAN HISTORY

987 Roma the goddess sitting with trophies.
998 Claudia, vestal virgin.
999 A vestal standing.
1037 Dacia restituta.

1038 Lucius Papirius.
1044 Tecialis, a high-priest.
1045 The Romans finding the books of the Sybils.
1046 Jugurtha, King of Numidia.

1048	Sophonisba taking poison, that she might not be taken in triumph of Rome.
1049	Clelia, a Roman lady, who was given as an hostage to Porsenna.
1053	Military charity.
1054	A conquered province.
1075	The death of Julius Caesar.
1076	Emperor Nero in the habit of a Muse.
1077	Emperor Domitian.
1078	Marcus Aurelius, on horseback.
1079	Antonia, wife of Germanicus.
1083	Romulus, first king of Rome.
1086	Numa Pompilius, as a priest.
1089	Lucius Junius Brutus.
1100	Pub. Cornelius Scipio Africanus.
1101	Attilius Regulus with a nail behind his neck.
1103	Lucius Quintus Cincinnatus.
1104	Marcus Portius Cato of Utica.
1111	Marcus Claudius Marcellus.
1118	Lucius Corn. Lentulus.
1122	Cato Censor.
1125	Marcus Tullius Cicero.
1126	The same.
1127	The same.
1142	Marcus Junius Brutus, with two daggers, and cap of liberty.
1143	Marcus Junius Brutus, with a dagger.
1160	Marcus Antonius and Cleopatra.
1165	Augustus.
1167	Livia, wife of Augustus.
1178	Tiberius.
1183	Nero Claudius Drusus, son of Livia, brother of Tiberius, father of Germanicus and Claudius Emperor.
1184	The same.
1198	Claudius.
1203	Nero.
1207	Poppea, wife of Nero.
1212	Otho.
1213	Vitellius.
1216	Vespasian.
1218	Titus.
1219	The same.
1223	Domitian.
1232	Trajan.
1233	Trajan, Plotina, Marciana, and Matilda.
1236	Marciana, sister of Trajan.
1239	Hadrian.
1241	Sabina.
1242	Sabina, wife of Hadrian.
1244	The same.
1246	Antinous, the favourite of Hadrian.
1256	Antoninus Pius.
1262	Gallerius Vallerius Antoninus, son of Antoninus Pius.
1263	Marcus Aurelius.
1264	The same.
1265	The same.
1266	Marcus Aurelius and Faustina.
1280	Commodus and Ennius Verus, brothers.
1281	Pertinax.
1294	Septimus Severus Julia Pia, Caracalla & Geta.
1302	Caracalla.
1306	Geta, brother of Caracalla.
1308	Diadumenus, son of Macrin.
1317	Alexander Severus.
1320	Maximinius.
1323	Gordianus Africanus.
1332	Philippus, Martia Otascilla his wife, & Philippus junior, his son.
1333	Trajanus Decius.
1345	Constantinus Magnus.
1351	Julian Apostate, and Flavia Julia Helena his wife.

1355	Cupid masked.	1454	A Sphynx.
1356	The same.	1457	A Lion.
1363	An Actor of Comedy.	1462	The same.
1402	Two Masks.	1465	A Lion devouring a wild Boar.
1408	A Chymera.	1467	A Lion devouring a Horse.
1421	A Man making a Vase.	1484	A Sow.
1422	The same.	1488	A Bull.
1423	The same.	1505	A Sea-horse.
1425	A Vase.	1518	Two Scorpions.
1433	A Vase.	1533	A Basilisk drawn by four Cocks.
1449	A Sphynx.		

ILLUSTRIOUS MEN

1538	Oliver Cromwell.	1544	Antonio Corregio.
1539	The Pretender.	1545	Rafael Urban.
1541	Titus Livius.	1546	Michael Angelo Buenaroti.
1543	Alexander Albanus.		

APPENDIX

1604	Neptune, *head.*	1623	A conquering Hero.
1605	Mercury, *figure.*	1624	A head of young Hercules.
1606	A Figure with a Vase, called a bathing Venus.	1625	A head of Hercules.
1607	Hercules gathering the golden Apples in the Gardens of the Hesperides.	1635	A Bacchanalian Triumph.
		1639	Leander in the Hellespont.
		1640	A crouching Venus.
1608	Paris, son of Priam, *head.*	1644	A Sacrifice.
1609	Pompey the Great, *head.*	1645	A Deification.
1610	Pompey the Great, less than the above.	1646	An Egyptian Figure, covered with Hieroglyphicks.
1612	George III.	1656	Marcus Tullius Cicero.
1613	An unknown Queen, in the King of France's cabinet.	1658	Diana, a large head.
		1660	Theon.
1614	Cleopatra.	1662	L. Q. Cincinnatus.
1617	Lucius Junius Brutus.	1671	Sir John Fielding.
1618	Four Masks.	1772	The Marriage of Bacchus and Ariadne.
1619	Earl of Clanbrassil.		
1620	Esculapius and Hygeia.	1673	Pope Clement XIV.
1621	Hygeia, &c. a Sacrifice, larger.	1674	The Marriage of Cupid and Psyche; in the cabinet of the Duke of Marlborough.
1622	The offering of Victory to a Trophy.		
		1675	Beautiful Medusa.

1676	Mercury standing, with a lyre.	1706	Louis XIV, *head*.
1677	Three Graces.	1707	Homer, *head*.
1678	Justice, with Scales and Cornucopia.	1708	Young Hercules, *head*.
1679	Hygeia, a figure.	1709	Phocion, *head*.
1680	A Man firing a Rocket, in the character of Mars.	1710	Female Hope, *figure*.
1681	Hygeia, with a basket of flowers.	1711	Cleopatra, *figure*.
1682	Hygeia, *figure*.	1712	Marcus Aurelius, *head*.
1683	Perseus and Andromeda.	1713	George III, *head*.
1684	Ajax guarding the body of Patroclus.	1714	Queen Charlotte, *head*.
1685	Sir Isaac Newton, *head*.	1715	Hercules stifling the Nemean Lion.
1686	The same.	1716	Countess of Portland, *head*.
1687	The same, smaller, from his own ring.	1717	Seneca, *a fine head*.
1688	Demosthenes, *head*.	1718	Mr. Hamilton of Bath, *head*.
1689	Milton, *head*.	1719	Shakespeare, *head*.
1690	Harpocrates, the God of Silence.	1720	The same, *head*.
1691	Henry IV of France, *head*.	1721	Mrs. Barbault, *head*.
1692	Duke de Sully, *head*.	1722	David Garrick, Esq. (Pingo).
1693	Louis XV of France, *head*.	1723	The same (Marchant).
1694	George II, *head*.	1724	The same (Kirk), *head*.
1695	Joseph II, Emperor of Germany, *head*.	1725	Dr. Mead, *head*.
1696	Oliver Cromwell, *head*.	1726	The same, smaller, *head*.
1697	Diana, *a large head*.	1727	Horus sitting upon the Lotus, with the sun and moon and other hieroglyphicks.
1698	Niobe, *head*.	1728	Neptune, *large head*.
1699	Alexander Pope, *head*.	1729	Mercury with a Caduseus, *head*.
1700	The same, *head*.	1730	Contemplating Muse, *figure*.
1701	Socrates, *head*.	1731	Hope, *head*.
1702	Head of a young Bacchus.	1732	The same, smaller, *head*.
1703	Antinous, *head*.	1733	Omphale, with the Club of Hercules.
1704	Sabina, *head*.	1734	Venus and Cupid on a Dolphin.
1705	Venus, *head*.	1735	Continence of Scipio, *figure*.

SECTION II

INTAGLIOS

The Improvements made in the Intaglios, since the publication of the First Edition of our Catalogue, require some Notice. We have found that many of them take a good

Polish, and when polished, have exactly the Effect of fine black Jasper; but this Operation must be performed with great Care, or the Work will essentially suffer by it. — Heads may be polished safely, and by this Means their Beauty be greatly increased: But figures scarcely admit of polishing, without Injury, unless there be such a Degree of Delicacy and Care observed, as would greatly enhance the Price.

We have also found out another Method of adding very considerably to the Beauty of these Intaglios, by polishing the Bezels, and giving a Ground of pale blue to the flat Surface of the Stone, which makes them greatly resemble the black and blue Onyxes, and equally ornamental for Rings or Seals.

They are also now made in a fine blue Jasper, that takes as good a Polish as Turquois Stone or Lapis Lazuli.

Though the superior Hardness, Sharpness, and Correctness of these Intaglios, place them far above all other Imitations or Copies of antique Gems, yet no Article, in the whole Extent of the fine Arts has ever been offered to the Public at so moderate a Price.

Those who favour us with Orders will please to mention both the Number and the Subject, to avoid Mistakes.

1	Dancing Fawn, *figure.*	24	Esculapius, *head.*
2	Mars and Venus, *figures.*	25	Germanicus, *head.*
3	The late Pope, *head.*	26	George II, *head.*
4	Diomedes, Apollo, and Eneas, *figures.*	27	Hygeia, *figure.*
		28	Adonis, *figure.*
5	Oliver Cromwell, *head.*	29	Horace, *head.*
6	Young Hercules, *head.*	30	Cicero, *head.*
7	A Victory holding a Pike, *figure.*	31	George III, *head.*
8	A Vestal, *figure.*	32	Henry IV of France, *head.*
9	Hercules and Lion, *figure.*	33	Conquered Province, *figure.*
10	Neptune, *head.*	34	Camillus, *head.*
11	Apollo, *head.*	35	Ceres, *head.*
12	Alexander Pope, *head.*	36	Socrates, *head.*
13	Medusa, *head.*	37	Olympias, *head.*
14	Homer, *head.*	38	A Fawn, *head.*
15	Scipio Africanus, *head.*	39	Ptolomy Philopater, *head.*
16	Socrates, *head.*	40	Sappho, *head.*
17	Marcus Aurelius, *head.*	41	Unknown Queen, perhaps Cleopatra, *head.*
18	Michael Angelo, *head.*	42	Minerva, *head.*
19	Sabina, *head.*	43	Theseus, *head.*
20	Sir Isaac Newton, *head.*	44	Charondas, *head.*
21	Lysimachus, *head.*	45	Philosopher, *head.*
22	Neptune, *head.*	46	Bacchus, *head.*
23	Ceres, *head.*		

47 Aristotle, *head.*
48 Hercules, *head.*
49 Periander, *head.*
50 Alexander Pope, *head.*
51 Sappho, *head.*
52 Juba, King of Mauritania, *head.*
53 Young Hercules, *head.*
54 Esculapius, *head.*
55 Perseus, *head.*
56 A Fawn, *head.*
57 A Lioness, *figure.*
58 Young Antoninus, *head.*
59 A Lion in front, *figure.*
60 Phocion, *head.*
61 Polyhimnia, muse of Rhetorick, *head.*
62 Iöle, *head.*
63 Mercury, son of Jupiter, *head.*
64 Drusus, son of Tiberius, *head.*
65 M. T. Cicero, *head.*
66 Laocoon, son of Priam, *head.*
67 Plato, *head.*
68 Atlas, supporting the World, *figure.*
69 A Lion devouring a Horse, *figure.*
70 Bacchus, *head.*
71 Esculapius, *head.*
72 Neptune, *head.*
73 Demosthenes, *head.*
74 Reposing Hercules, *figure.*
75 Cupid holding a Bow, *figure.*
76 A Vase, *figure.*
77 Aristophanes, Poet, *head.*
78 Horace, *head.*
79 Solon, *head.*
80 Virgil, *head.*
81 Young Faustina, *head.*
82 Didia Clara, daughter of Didius Julianus, *head.*
83 Neptune, *head.*
84 Hercules and Iöle, *heads.*
85 Contemplative Muse, *figure.*

86 Sabina, wife of Hadrian, in the character of Ceres, *head.*
87 Pompey, *head.*
88 Cupid, burning a Butterfly, *figure.*
89 A Child with a Cat, *figure.*
90 Poppea, wife of Nero, *head.*
91 Leander, *head.*
92 Britannicus, son of Claudius, *head.*
93 Paris, son of Priam, *head.*
94 Theseus raising a stone &c., *figure.*
95 A Sphynx, *figure.*
96 Sir Isaac Newton, small, from a ring that belonged to himself, *head*
97 Chiron shooting with a bow, *figure.*
98 Oliver Cromwell, from a ring in the possession of Sir Thomas Frankland, *head.*
99 Jupiter Amnon, small, *head.*
100 Alexander Pope, *head.*
101 Diomedes, *figure.*
102 Venus, *head.*
103 Venus and Cupid, *figures.*
104 A Sow, *figure.*
105 A Sphynx, *figure.*
106 Chiron, Centaur, *head.*
107 Apollo, *head.*
108 Pan, *head.*
109 Lucius Junius Brutus, *head.*
110 A figure from Herculaneum.
111 Alexander Medicis, *head.*
112 Augustus Caesar, *head.*
113 Lucius Verus, *head.*
114 Unknown, *head.*
115 Julius Caesar and Livia, *heads.*
116 Pope, *head.*
117 Scantilla, wife of Didius Julianus, *small head.*
118 Man making a Vase, *figure.*
119 Antinous, *head.*
120 Ceres, small, *head.*

PLATE VII

Wedgwood Red Mark Bone China 1812 to 1828. Rare free-hand decorated plate, cup and saucer, possibly painted by Aaron Steele, and named on reverse 'Sheildrake', 'Crossbill', and 'Heron'

121 The Centaur Nessus, bound by Love, *figures.*
122 Apollo standing with his lyre, *figure.*
123 Juno upon an Eagle, *figure.*
124 Bacchante, *figure.*
125 Sacrifice, *figure.*
126 Cupid and Psyche, *figures.*
127 Mercury standing, *figure.*
128 The three Graces, *figures.*
129 Mercury, *figure.*
130 Mercury sitting on a Ram, *figure.*
131 Mercury, God of Travellers, *figure.*
132 Mercury raising a dead Man by the hand, *figures.*
133 Mercury keeping the flock of Admetus, *figures.*
134 Cupid and Psyche, *figures.*
135 Harpocrates, *head.*
136 Ditto standing in a Bark, *figure.*
137 Ditto with Cornucopia, *figure.*
138 Ditto.
139 Jupiter Conservator, *figure.*
140 Three Graces, *figures.*
141 Dr. Mead, large, *head.*
142 Plutarch, *head.*
143 A furious Fawn, *figure.*
144 Julius Caesar, *figure.*
145 Jupiter, Hebe, and Ganymede, *figures.*
146 Venus, *head.*
147 Bacchanalian figures.
148 Venus Victrix, *figure.*
149 An Egyptian figure.
150 Three Graces, *figures.*
151 Peace, or Union of Hands.
152 Neptune with Sea-horses, *figures.*
153 Pomona, *figures.*
154 Phaeton falling from Heaven, *figure.*
155 The Lyre of Apollo.

156 Thalia, Muse of Comedy, *figure.*
157 Euterpe with two flutes, *figure.*
158 Melpomene with a mask, *figure.*
159 Terpsichore, Muse, *figure.*
160 Apollo and Lyre, *figure.*
161 Diana Huntress, *figure.*
162 Endymion with the Moon, *figure.*
163 Bacchus with a Fawn, *figures.*
164 Bacchus sitting on a Tyger, *figures.*
165 Hercules overcome by Love, *figure*
166 Venus and Cupid, *figures.*
167 The Temple of Venus.
168 Cupid, *figure.*
169 Esculapius, *figure.*
170 Enchantment, *figures.*
171 Aesop, *head.*
172 Pythagorus, sitting, *figure.*
173 Hero and Leander.
174 Perseus standing, *figure.*
175 Meleager with a boar's head, *figure.*
176 Claudia, Vestal Virgin, *figure.*
177 Castor and Pollux.
178 Roman Matron, *figure.*
179 Antonia and Urn.
180 Seneca in the Bath, *figure.*
181 Constantine on horseback, *figure.*
182 A Man putting on a Mask, *figure.*
183 Cupid masked, *figure.*
184 Cupid dressing a Mask, *figure.*
185 A Chimaera.
186 A Man making a Vase, *figure.*
187 A vase.
188 A Cock with the Diamonds.
189 Titus Livius, *head.*
190 Baron Montesquieu, *head.*
191 Corregio, *head.*
192 Raphael, *head.*
193 Carlo Maratti, *head.*
194 Chiron, the Centaur, playing upon the Lyre, *figures.*

195 Semiramis giving command to her son, *figure.*
196 Alcibiades, *head.*
197 Hannibal, *head.*
198 Prometheus forming a Man, *figure.*
199 Theseus killing the Minotaur, *figure.*
200 Medea, &c., *figures.*
201 Lewis XV of France, *head.*
202 Jupiter Olympus, *head.*
203 Cicero, *head.*
204 Homer, *head.*
205 Scaevola, &c., *figures.*
206 Hope, *figure.*
207 Venus and Cupid, *figures.*
208 Cupid and Psyche, *figures.*
209 Iöle, *head.*
210 David Garrick, *head.*
211 Cleopatra, *figure.*
212 Milton, *head.*
213 Regulus with a Nail, *head.*
214 Emperor of Germany, *head.*
215 Jupiter with all his Attributes, *head.*
216 Birth of Bacchus, of Michael Angelo's Seal, *figures.*
217 A Cow and Calf, *figures.*
218 Aegle binding Silenus to a Tree, *figures.*
219 Sophonisba taking poison, *figure.*
220 Caliope, Muse of heroic Poesy, *figure.*
221 Diana Huntress, *figure.*
222 Papirius and his Mother, *figures.*
223 Marcus Junius Brutus, *head.*
224 Iöle, *head.*
225 Henry IV of France, *head.*
226 Lewis XIV, *head.*
227 Anacreon, Poet, *head.*
228 Agatho, *head.*
229 Hypocrates, *head.*
230 Caius Ennius, Latin poet, *head.*

231 Lucius Apuleius, *head.*
232 Hermes, Trismegistus, *head.*
233 Ovid, Poet, *head.*
234 Theocritus, Poet, *head.*
235 Pythagoras, *head.*
236 Socrates, *head.*
237 Portrait of a gentleman, *head.*
238 Medusa, *head.*
239 Seneca, *head.*
240 Alexander, *head.*
241 Minerva, *figure.*
242 Marcus Aurelius on horseback, *figure.*
243 Iöle, *figure.*
244 Peace, *figures.*
245 Jupiter and Leda, *figures.*
246 Mars, *figure.*
247 Bacchanalian figures.
248 Neptune standing in a shell, *figure.*
249 Cicero, *head.*
250 A Bacchante with a Thirsis, *figure,*
251 Bacchus and Ariadne on a Tyger. *figures.*
252 Saturn with an encircled Serpent, *figure.*
253 Cybele, wife of Saturn, *head.*
254 Saturn devouring a stone, *figure.*
255 Cybele, wife of Saturn, *head.*
256 The Flower Lotus.
257 Belerophon watering Pegasus, *figure.*
258 Isis with the Cystrum, *head.*
259 Canopus, *figure.*
260 Jupiter and Isis.
261 Isis with the budding Horns, *head.*
262 Ganymede, *figure.*
263 Virgil, *head.*
264 Dr. Mead, small, *head.*
265 George II, *head.*
266 Madona, *head.*
267 Shakespeare, *head.*

268	Two Cupids, *figures.*	308	Priam begging the body of Hector from Achilles, *figures.*
269	Mr. Pope, *head.*		
270	Mars and Venus, small, *figures.*	309	Esculapius, *figure.*
271	Apollo, large, *head.*	310	Hygia, *figure.*
272	Venus, *figure.*	311	Sacerdotus, *figure.*
273	Conquered Province, second size, *figure.*	312	Neptune, *figure.*
		313	A Sacrifice, *figure.*
274	Apollo, *figure.*	314	Virtue, *figure.*
275	Doctor Lucas, *head.*	315	Justice, *figure.*
276	Madona, *head.*	316	Neptune in peace with Minerva, *figures.*
277	Mars.		
278	Venus, *figure.*	317	Musius Seaevola before Porsenna, *figure.*
279	Hygia, *figure.*		
280	David Garrick, *head.*	318	Ulysses stopping the chariot of Victory, *figures.*
281	Venus, *figure.*		
282	Three Graces, *figures.*	319	A Sacrifice, *figures.*
283	R.H. Duke of Gloucester, *head.*	320	Diana, *figure.*
284	Sir Isaac Newton, *head.*	321	Ceres instructing Tripolemus in Agriculture, *figures.*
285	Britannicus, *head.*		
286	Duke de Sully, *head.*	322	Flora, *figure.*
287	Priestess, *figure.*	323	Sophonisba taking Poison, *figure.*
288	Minerva.	324	Plato.
289	Hygia, *figure.*	325	A Pointer dog.
290	Diana of the Mountains, *figure.*	326	Hope with an Anchor, *figure.*
291	George III, *head.*	327	Two Seahorses, *figures.*
292	Diana, *figure.*	328	A Lion seizing a Horse, *figures.*
293	Apollo and Daphne, *figures.*	329	Pindar, *head.*
294	Hercules killing the Minataur, *figures.*	330	Cybele giving Jupiter to be educated, *figures.*
		331	A Warrior, *figure.*
295	Venus, *head.*	332	Hercules killing a Bull, *figures.*
296	Pomona, *figure.*	333	Mucius Scaevola burning his hand &c., *figure.*
297	Venus, *head.*		
298	Saturn, *figure.*	334	Diogenes disputing with Lais, *figures.*
299	Venus Victrix, *figures.*		
300	Offering to Victory, *figures.*	335	A Sacrifice, *figures.*
301	Diomede or Perseus, *figures.*	336	Neptune, *head.*
302	Agrippina.	337	A Warrior, *figures.*
303	A Bull.	338	Ditto, *figures.*
304	Hannibal, *head.*	339	A Bird let fly.
305	Neptune, *figure.*	340	Hygia, *figure.*
306	Night shedding Poppies, *figures.*	341	George III, *head.*
307	Nereides, *figures.*		

342	A Cupid, *figure*.	359	A gaping head.
343	Alphabetical Cypher.	360	Mrs. Barbault, *head*.
344	Offering to Victory, *figure*.	361	Duke of Richmond, *head*.
345	Perseus with Armour, small, *figure*.	362	Abundantia, *figure*.
346	Venus Victrix, *figure*.	363	Shakespeare, *head*.
347	Silence, *head*.	364	The Bath Washerwoman, *head*.
348	Venus and Cupid, *figures*.	365	A Brace of Birds.
349	Cupid with a Caduceus, *figure*.	366	The Queen, *head*.
350	A piping Bacchus and Cupid, *figures*.	367	Cato, *head*.
351	A Cupid with a Butterfly, *figure*.	368	Present Pope, *head*.
352	Esculapius, Hygia, and Telephorus *figures*.	369	Their Majesties, *heads*.
353	Three Cupids, *figures*.	370	Cervantes, *head*.
354	Marriage of Cupid and Psyche, *figures*.	371	William III, *head*.
355	Two Cupids in a Bark, *figures*.	372	Garrick, *head*.
356	Lord Chatham, *head*.	373	Another, *head*.
357	Milton, *head*.	374	Mason's Arms.
358	Zingara, *head*.	375	Horse taking a Leap, *figure*.
		376	Xenophon, *head*.
		377	Flora, *figure*.
		378	Buchanan, *head*.
		379	Female Fortune, *figure*.

Many of these Seals are made with Shanks of the same Stone, highly polished, and particularly a complete Set of Cyphers, consisting of all the Combinations of two Letters: These require no mounting, but may be finished with gold or gilt Ornaments, according to the Taste of Purchasers.

* * *

We beg leave in this Place to observe, that if Gentlemen or Ladies choose to have Models of themselves, Families, or Friends, made in Wax, or engraven in Stones, of proper Sizes for Seals, Rings, Lockets, or Bracelets, they may have as many durable Copies of those Models as they please, either in Cameo or Intaglio, for any of the above Purposes, at a moderate Expence: and this Nation is at present happy in the Possession of severals Artists of distinguished Merit, as engravers, and Modellers, who are capable of executing these fine Works with great Delicacy and Precision.

If the Nobility and Gentry of *Great Britain* should please to encourage this Design, they will not only procure to themselves *everlasting Portraits*, but have the Pleasure of giving Life and Vigour to the Arts of Modelling and Engraving. — The Art of making *durable Copies*, at a small Expence, will thus promote the Art of *making Originals*, and future Ages may view the Productions of the Age of George III with the same Veneration that we now gaze upon those of Alexander and Augustus.

Nothing can contribute more effectually to diffuse a good Taste through the Arts, than the Power of multiplying Copies of fine Things, in Materials fit to be applied for Ornaments; by which Means the public Eye is instructed; bad and good Works are nicely distinguished, and all the Arts receive Improvement: nor can there be any surer Way of rendering an exquisite Piece, possessed by an Individual, famous, without diminishing the Value of an Original: for the more Copies there are of any Works, as of the Venus Medicis for instance, the more celebrated the Original will be, and the more Honour derived to the Possessor. Every body wishes to see the Original of a beautiful Copy.

A Model of a Portrait in Wax, when it is of a proper Size for a Seal, Ring, or Bracelet, will cost about *Three Guineas*; and of a Portrait, from three to six Inches Diameter, Three, Four, or Five Guineas.

Any Number of Copies, not fewer than ten, we propose to make in *Intaglio*, in Black and Blue Onyxes for Seals or Rings, at 5s. each.

Any Number of *Cameos* for Rings, not fewer than ten, at the same Price.

Any Number of *Cameos* for Bracelets, not fewer than ten, at 7s. 6d. each.

Any Number of *Portraits* from three to six Inches Diameter, not fewer than ten, at 10s. 6d. each.

The Cameos will be made of the artificial Jasper, with coloured Grounds, the Colours penetrating the whole Mass, like those of a natural Stone, a new Composition, little inferior to the Onyx.

CLASS II

BAS-RELIEFS, MEDALLIONS, CAMEO-MEDALLIONS, TABLETS, &c.

CHIEFLY CLASSICAL SUBJECTS

The Articles in this Class may be made either in the *black Basaltes*, which has the Appearance of antique Bronze, or in the *blue and white Jasper*.

These Bas-reliefs may be applied as Cabinet Pictures, or for ornamenting Cabinets, Book-Cases, Writing-Tables, &c. The large *Cameo-Pictures*, and *Tablets* for Chimney-Pieces, in blue and white Jasper, have been brought to their present Degree of Perfection with much Labour and Expence to the Artist, and may with Propriety have a Place amongst the finest Ornaments the Arts have produced; *no Cameos, Medallions, or Bas-reliefs*, so highly finished, and of equal Magnitude, having ever been made in such durable and exquisite Materials.

It may be proper to observe here, that this artificial Jasper is made in two Colours; the Relief of one Colour and the Ground of another, which is not laid upon the Surface like Enamel, but goes thro' the whole Mass; and that the Grounds admit of a good Polish; so that those who prefer a bright to a mat Surface, may have Pictures and Bas-reliefs from the Size of a Ring to that of a large *Chimney-piece tablet* or *Cameo Picture*, of eighteen or twenty Inches Diameter, that in Polish, Colour, and Delicacy, will be little inferior to the finest *Onyx*.

The following List will shew, that the Articles of this Class have already been considerably extended, both in Number and Size; and we flatter ourselves, the Additions we are daily making to it, will farther recommend this Collection to the Notice of our generous Patrons, and of all liberal Artists, who may have Opportunities of applying these Ornaments in a proper Manner.

The same Subjects may also be made in a hard, but cheap light-coloured *Terra Cotta*, that may be gilt, varnished, or painted in Oil Colours, suitable to the Apartments in which they are used.

1 Birth of Bacchus, 6 inches by 5.
2 The War of Jupiter and the Titans, oval, 9 inches by 6.
3 The destruction of Niobe's Children, 9 inches by 6.
4 The Feast of the Gods, ditto.
5 The Marriage Supper of Perseus and Andromeda, ditto.
6 An antique Boar Hunting, ditto.
7 Jupiter and Ganymede, in a long Square, 6 inches by 3.
8 Apollo and Marsyas, octagon, 7 inches by 6 (Landre).
9 Apollo and Daphne, ditto.
10 Apollo and Python, ditto.
11 Judgment of Midas, ditto.
12 Bacchanalian Triumph, 6 inches by 4, square and oval.
13 Bacchanalian Boys at Play, oval, 8 inches by 6.
14 Silenus and Boys, its companion, same size.
15 Boys dancing round a Tree, round, 6 inches diameter.
16 Bacchus and Panther, either upon an oval or square tablet 11 inches by 6.
17 A head of Venus, round, 2 inches diameter.
18 A head of Apollo, oval, 2 inches by 1½.
19 Minerva, oval, 6 inches by 5.
20 Alexander, 2 inches by 1½.
21 Minerva, 2½ inches by 2.
22 Perseus, 4¾ inches by 4 inches.
23 Andromeda, its companion, same size.
24 Young Hercules, 2¾ inches by 2.
25 Young Hercules, 4½ inches by 3¾.
26 Hercules and Omphale, 3 inches by 2½.
27 Cupid shaving his Bow, 3 inches by 2¼.
28 Sacrifice to Esculapius, 4 inches by 3½.
29 The Graces by M. Burch, from an Etruscan Bas-relief in Sir W. Hamilton's cabinet at the British Museum. (M. Burch)

30 The Marriage of Cupid and Psyche, enlarged from the Gem in the cabinet of his Grace the Duke of Marlborough, 3 inches by 2¼.

Ditto, 8¼ inches by 6½.
Ditto, 10 inches by 7½.
Ditto, 12 inches by 8.
Ditto, 14 inches by 10.
Ditto, 16 inches by 11½.

31 The Judgement of Paris, 3 inches by 2½.
32 Boys playing with a Goat, 4¾ inches by 3¾.
33 Cassandra, a fine figure in high relief, 7¼ inches by 4½. (Bacon)
34 Diomede, with the Palladium. (Bacon)
35 Bacchanalian Boys, 5 inches by 3½.
36 Ditto, its companion.
37 A Bacchanalian Female and Children, 8 inches by 6.
38 A Fawn, Youth, 9 inches by 7.
39 Ditto, Adolescence, same size.
40 Ditto, Manhood, ditto.
41 Ditto, Old Age, ditto.
42 Farnesian Hercules, high relief in Cameo, 4 inches by 3.
43 Omphale, ditto.
44 Apollo, ditto.
45 Piping Fawn, ditto.
46 Venus, ditto.
47 Adonis, ditto.
48 Ceres, ditto.
49 Venus Belsesses, ditto.
50 Althea, the mother of Meleager, burning the Firebrand, 3½ inches by 2½.
51 Herculaneum dancing Nymph, 10 inches by 7¾.
52 Ditto
53 Ditto
54 Ditto   10 inches by 7¾.
55 Ditto
56 Ditto
57 Centaur, round tablet, 11½ inches diameter.
58 Ditto.
59 Ditto.
60 — — Polyphemus, ditto.
61 Marsyas and young Olympus, ditto.
62 Papyrius and his Mother, ditto
64 A Bacchanalian Figure from Herculaneium, upon a round tablet, ditto.
65 Ditto.

66 Venus Belsesses, oval tablet, 10½ inches by 7¾.
67 Zeno, ditto.
68 Cupid reposing, 3 inches by 2½. (Parker)
69 Judgment of Hercules, an oval tablet, 15 inches by 11.
   Ditto, 12 inches by 8.
   Ditto, 14 inches by 9.
   Ditto, 16 inches by 12.
70 Bacchanalian Triumph, long square tablet, 21 inches by 9.
71 Bacchanalian Sacrifice, ditto.
72 Death of a Roman Warrior, ditto, 20 inches by 11.
73 A Lion from the antique, 4½ inches by 3½.
74 Perseus and a Centaur, 4 inches by 3½.
75 Hercules and Theseus supporting the World, or the power of union, 4 inches by 3¼.
76 Head of an old Satyr, in a fine style, and highly finished, 6 inches by 4½.
77 Night, 7 inches by 5½.
78 Day, its companion, ditto.
79 Night, 20 inches by 14½.
80 Day, its companion, ditto.
81 Meleager and Atalanta killing the Caledonian Boar, 7 inches by 6.
82 A Bull finely modelled from the antique, ¾ inches by 2½.
83 Jupiter and Semele, oval, 3 inches by 2.
84 Hunting.
85 Ditto.
86 Music.
87 The Arts.
88 Venus and Cupid with the emblem of fire, large oval medallion. (Grant & Hoskins)
89 Venus and Cupid, with the emblem of air.
90 Venus and Cupid, with the emblem of earth.
91 Venus and Cupid, with the emblem of water.
92
93 Lyre and two Sphynxes, a tablet for ditto.
94 Large Head of Medusa, round, 5 inches.
95 Another model, oval, 3 inches.
96 Another profile, with wings, 2 inches by 1½.
97 Another profile, 2 inches by 1½.
98 Jupiter, oval, 8 inches by 6 (Flaxman).
99 Juno, ditto, 8 inches by 6. (Flaxman)
100 Apollo, oval, 8 inches by 6 (Flaxman)
101 A Muse, ditto, 8 inches by 6. (Flaxman)
102 Contemplative Muse, 8 inches by 6. (Flaxman)

103 Hercules strangling the Lion, 8 inches by 6. (Flaxman)

104 Hercules binding Cerberus, 8 inches by 6. (Flaxman)

105 Meleager, 8 inches by 6. (Flaxman)

106 Justice, oval, 7 inches by $5\frac{1}{2}$ (Flaxman)

107 Minerva, ditto. (Flaxman)

108 Hope, ditto. (Flaxman)

109 Melpomene, 8 inches by 6. (Flaxman)

110 Comedy, ditto. (Flaxman)

111 A dancing Nymph, oval, ditto. (Flaxman)

112 Bacchus, a head, bas-relief, oval, ditto. (Flaxman)

113 Ariadne, a head, 8 inches by 6. (Flaxman)

114 Spring, a head, bas-relief, 10 inches by 8. (Flaxman)

115 Summer, ditto. (Flaxman)

116 Autumn, ditto. (Flaxman)

117 Winter, ditto. (Flaxman)

118 Birth of Bacchus, oval, bas-relief, $7\frac{1}{2}$ inches by $5\frac{3}{4}$. (Hackwood)

119 Isis, a head, 3 inches by $2\frac{1}{2}$. (Flaxman)

120 Ariadne, ditto, 2 inches by $1\frac{3}{4}$. (Flaxman)

121 Bacchus, ditto, same size. (Flaxman)

122 Pan, head, 3 inches by $2\frac{1}{2}$. (Flaxman)

123 Syrinx, ditto, same size. (Flaxman)

124 Perseus and Andromeda, 6 inches by 5. (Flaxman)

125 Indian Bacchus, matches 76. (Hackwood)

126
127
128 } Bacchanalian figures, 6 inches by 4. (Landre)
129
130

131 Lion and two Boys, $7\frac{1}{4}$ inches by $5\frac{1}{2}$.

132 Lion and three boys, 5 inches by $3\frac{3}{4}$.

133 Mask, head, round, $2\frac{1}{2}$ inches.

134 Ditto.

135 Cupid and Hymen, 5 inches by $3\frac{1}{2}$. (Grant & Hoskins)

136 Cupid burning a Butterfly, 5 inches by $3\frac{1}{2}$. (Grant & Hoskins)

137 A Philosopher reading on the immortality of the soul, $3\frac{1}{4}$ inches by $2\frac{1}{4}$. (Landre)

138 Dead Jesus, with the Virgin and Boys, $3\frac{3}{4}$ inches by $3\frac{1}{3}$. (Landre)

139 Pan reposing with young Satyrs, 8 inches by 6.

140 Fawns sacrificing, tablet, 15 inches by $8\frac{1}{2}$. (Flaxman)

141 Esculapius. (Flaxman)

142 Hygia. (Flaxman)

143 Vestal. (Flaxman)

144 Artemesia. (Flaxman)

145 Boy riding upon a Lion. (Flaxman)
146 Indian Bacchus, bas-relief figure, 4 inches by 3. (Flaxman)
147 Roman Matron, ditto. (Flaxman.)
148 Sophonisba, ditto. (Flaxman)
149 Hercules, ditto. (Flaxman)
150 Piping Fawn, ditto. (Flaxman)
151 Abundantia, ditto. (Flaxman)
152 Medea, ditto. (Flaxman)
153 Bacchanalian Triumph, oval tablet, $9\frac{3}{4}$ inches by $7\frac{1}{2}$. (Flaxman)
154 An autique male Figure, with a Greyhound, holding a seal upon his lips, 9 inches high. (Flaxman)
155 Hebe and the Eagle, 7 inches by $4\frac{1}{2}$. (Flaxman)
156 Venus Belsesses, 7 inches.
157 Hercules Farnesis, $7\frac{1}{4}$ inches.
158 Sacrificing figure, 7 inches.
159 Vestal, 4 inches.
160 Juno, $4\frac{1}{4}$ inches. (Flaxman)
161 Euterpe, $4\frac{1}{4}$ inches. (Flaxman)
162 Female figure and Urn, $4\frac{1}{4}$ inches.
163 Fame, &c., $4\frac{1}{4}$ inches. (Flaxman)
164 Conquered Province, 11 inches by 7. (Stephan)
  { Ditto, 3 inches by $2\frac{1}{2}$.
  { Ditto, round, $8\frac{3}{4}$ inches.
165 Head of Flora, 9 inches by 8. (Flaxman)
166 Sleeping Venus cloathed, 4 inches by 11. (Flaxman)
167 Priestess, $6\frac{3}{4}$ inches.
168 Venus and Cupid, 5 inches by 4.
169 Diomede, $4\frac{1}{4}$ inches by $4\frac{1}{4}$. (Flaxman)
170 Ariadne drawn by Panthers, with Pan, &c., $10\frac{1}{2}$ inches by $14\frac{1}{4}$. (Flaxman)
171 A Sacrifice to Peace, $3\frac{3}{4}$ inches by $2\frac{3}{4}$.
172 Groupe of four female figures, 9 inches by 10.
173 Sacrifice, 10 inches by 14.
174 Bacchanalian piece, 8 inches by $10\frac{1}{2}$.
175)
176 |
177 }Bas-reliefs (by John of Bolognia)
178)
179 By the same.
180
181 Winged Cupid upon a Swan, $2\frac{1}{4}$ inches by $2\frac{1}{2}$. (Flaxman)
182 Winged Cupid flying away with a Swan, ditto. (Flaxman)
183 Judgment of Paris, 5 inches by 6. (Flaxman)

184 Vulcan with Mars and Venus in the Net, ditto.
185 Rape of Helen, ditto.
186 Death of Adonis, ditto.
187 Bathing Nymphs, &c. ditto.
188 Goats, 5 inches by 3¾.
189 Triumph of Silenus, from a gem. (Flaxman)
190 Triumph of Bacchanalian Boys, 2 inches by 1½.
191
192 } Procession of little Boys, &c., 2 inches by 5 or 6.
193 Four Boys at play, 5 inches by 3¾.
194 Three ditto, its companion.
195 Panther and Bacchanalian Boys, 10 inches by 7½.
196 Sacrifice to Hymen, to match No. 30. (Flaxman)
197 Andromache, round, 8½ inches. (Bacon)
198 Flora, ditto, 10 inches. (Bacon)
199 Ditto, 17 inches by 7½.
    Ditto, 19 inches by 8¼.
200 Sacrifice to Bacchus, 19 inches by 8¼.
    Ditto, 22 inches by 9½.
201 Triumph of ditto, 14 inches by 6½. (Hackwood)
    Ditto, oval, 10 inches by 7¼.
202 Apotheosis of Homer, 14 inches by 7½. (Flaxman)
203 Nine Muses, 25 inches by 8. (Flaxman)
204 Muses with Apollo, in two tablets, 18 inches by 6. (Flaxman)
205 Dancing Hours, 18 inches by 6. (Flaxman)
    Ditto, 1(?)¾ inches by 5¼.
206 Birth of Bacchus, from M. Angelo's seal, 23 inches by 11.
    Ditto, 27 inches by 12.
207 Triumph of Love.
208 Sacrifice to Love, 21 inches by 9½.
    Ditto, 25 inches by 10½.
209 Triumph of Venus, 17 inches by 8.
    Ditto, 20 inches by 9.
210 Hero and Leander, 17 inches by 8.
    Ditto, 20 inches by 9.
211 Priam begging the body of Hector from Achilles, 14 inches by 11½.
    Ditto, 17½ inches by 13.
212 Triumph of Bacchus and Ariadne, 23 inches by 9½.
    Ditto, 26 inches by 10¾.
213 Boys and Goat, &c. Bacchanalians, 11½ inches by 7.
    Ditto, oval, 12¾ inches by 9.

214 Nine Muses and Apollo, separate, 8 inches by $5\frac{1}{2}$.
Ditto, $3\frac{1}{2}$ inches by $2\frac{1}{2}$.
215 Young Hercules, $6\frac{1}{4}$ inches by 4.
216 Ganymede and Eagle, 5 inches by 4.
217 Meleager and Atalanta killing the Calydonian Boar, 15 inches by $6\frac{1}{4}$.
Ditto, oval, $11\frac{1}{4}$ inches by 8.
218 Tragedy, Comedy and Apollo, $9\frac{1}{2}$ inches by 6. (Flaxman)
219 A Horse, $5\frac{3}{8}$ inches by $4\frac{1}{2}$. (Mrs. Landre)
220 Bacchus with an Urn and Grapes, $3\frac{3}{8}$ inches by $2\frac{3}{4}$.
221 Boys at play, $3\frac{3}{8}$ inches by $2\frac{3}{4}$.
Ditto, $3\frac{3}{8}$ inches by $2\frac{3}{4}$.
222 Four Seasons, 4 inches by $3\frac{3}{8}$. (Flaxman)
Ditto, 2 inches by $1\frac{1}{2}$.

CLASS III

KINGS AND ILLUSTRIOUS PERSONS OF ASIA, EGYPT AND GREECE

The peculiar Fitness of our Compositions for rendering exact and durable Copies of antique Medallions, Heads of illustrious Men, &c. at a moderate Price, has induced us to aim at a *Biographical Catalogue* of distinguished Characters, for the Illustration of that pleasing and instructive Branch of History; and with this View we have been at a very considerable Expence in collecting, repairing, and modelling Portraits of illustrious Men of various Ages and Countries; and the following Lists will shew, that besides an extensive *mythological Cabinet*, we can furnish a Suite of *Grecian* and *Roman* History, from the Time of the *Trojan* War, to the Removal of the Seat of the *Roman* Empire to *Constantinople*.

The Thread of History is continued by a Set of the *Popes* near *compleat*, and all the Kings of *England* and *France*; and the more recent Periods of History are illustrated by a considerable Number of *Poets*, *Painters*, and other famous Persons, from *Chaucer* to the present Time.

SECTION I

KINGS AND QUEENS OF ASIA MINOR, GREECE, &c.

BEFORE CHRIST

1	Ariadne.	4	Iphigenia.
2	Helena.	5	Cassandra.
3	Polyxena, daughter of Priam.	6	Dido.

220

7	Amyntas, King of Macedonia.	20	Nicomedes, King of Bythinia.
8	Ariobarzanes Eusebius, King of Pontus.	21	Ariobarzanes Philorum, King of Pontus.
9	Maufolus, King of Caria.	22	Antiochus Theos, King of Syria.
10	Artemesia, Queen of Caria.	23	Antiochus Hierax.
11	Alexander the Great.	24	Antiochus Magnus, King of Syria.
12	Alexander and Olympia.	25	Ariarethes V, King of Cappadocia.
13	Alexander Epirota.	26	Brusias, King of Bythinia.
14	Ptolomy Lagus I, King of Egypt.	27	Ptolomy Evergetes, or Physcon, King of Egypt.
15	Seleucus Nicanor, King of Syria.	28	Antiochus Cyricenes, King of Syria.
16	Antigonus, King of Asia.	29	Antiochus Grippus and Cleopatra.
17	Demetrius Poliorcetes, King of Macedonia.	30	Philippus Epiphanes, King of Syria.
18	Lysimachus, King of Macedonia.	31	Ariarethes X, King of Cappadocia.
19	Arsinoe, his widow.		

SECTION II

STATESMEN, PHILOSOPHERS AND ORATORS OF GREECE

BEFORE CHRIST

1	Minos, King and Lawgiver of Crete.	19	Aristomachus, lover of Bees.
2	Theseus, founder of the republic of Athens.	20	Demosthenes, Orator.
3	Lycurgus, Lawgiver of Sparta.	21	Epaminondas, Theban general.
4	Bias, Phil. of Pirene.	22	Mago and Dionysius of Utica.
5	Pittacus, King and Phil. of Lesbos.	23	Hypocrates.
6	Chilo, Phil. of Lacedemon.	24	Democritus.
7	Solon, Lawgiver of Athens.	25	Archytus, mathematician of Tarentum.
8	Thales, Phil. of Milletus.	26	Plato.
9	Heraclitus.	27	Leodamus.
10	Pythagoras.	28	Isocrates.
11	Aristides.	29	Eschines.
12	Socrates.	30	Calysthenes.
13	Zaleucus, Lawgiver of Locri.	31	Diogenes.
14	Lysander, Admiral of Lacedemon.	32	Aristotle, two models.
15	Antisthenes.	33	Xenocrates.
16	Thrasibulus, Athenian General.	34	Epicurus.
17	Conon.	35	Euclid.
18	Aristippus.	36	Theophrastus.

37	Crates.	42	Apuleius, rhetorician.
38	Aratus.	43	Carniades, philosopher.
39	Zeno, stoic.	44	Asclepiades.
40	Archimedes.	45	Possidonius, mathematician.
41	Chrysippus.	46	Apoloneus Tyaneus.

ADDITIONS

BEFORE CHRIST

47	Herodotus, historian.	49	Xenophon, historian and philosopher.
48	Thucydides, historian.		

SECTION III

POETS

BEFORE CHRIST

1	Pytheus, poet of Colophon.	9	Euripides.
2	Hesiod.	10	Sophocles.
3	Homer.	11	Aristophanes.
4	Alceus.	12	Menander.
5	Sappho.	13	Posidippus.
6	Anacreon.	14	Theocritus.
7	Simonides.	15	Apoloneus of Rhodes.
8	Pindar.	16	Moschus.

SECTION IV

GRECIAN HEADS OF LARGER MODELS

OR SUCH AS HAVE BEEN MADE SINCE THE ABOVE CLASSES WERE FORMED.

1	Homer, $3\frac{1}{2}$ inches by 2.	8	Alexander, ditto.
2	Socrates, ditto.	9	Lycurgus, ditto.
3	Pittacus, ditto.	10	Plato, ditto.
4	Alexander, ditto.	11	Demosthenes, ditto.
5	Minos, 4 inches by 3.	12	Herodotus, 3 inches by $2\frac{1}{2}$.
6	Cyrus, ditto.	13	Thucidides, ditto.
7	Lysimachus, ditto.	14	Zenophon, ditto.

THE ANCIENT ROMAN HISTORY

from the Foundation of the City to the End of the Consular-Government, including the Age of Augustus; in a regular Series of 60 medals from DASSIER. Notwithstanding the great Difficulty in *moulding* and *firing* these Medals *with their Reverses*, they are sold at 6d. a Piece.

1   The Head of Romulus.
      Reverse, Foundation of Rome.
2   Rape of the Sabines.
3   The Head of Numa.
4   The Combat of the Horatii and Curatii.
      Reverse, Alba subdued.
5   Oath of Brutus.
      Reverse, Rome free under the Consuls.
6   The Head of Brutus.
      Reverse, Brutus, as Judge, commanding his Son to be put to death.
7   The Valour of Horatius Cocles.
      Reverse, Constancy of Scaevola.
8   The Return of the People to Rome from the Sacred Mount.
      Reverse, the Creation of Tribunes.
9   Coriolanus.
      Reverse, Filial Submission.
10   The zeal of the Fabians.
      Reverse, a Dictator from the Plough.
11   The Twelve Tables.
      Reverse, the Death of Virginia.
12   Creation of Censors.
      Reverse, Censors, surrounded with the People.
13   Generosity of the Roman Ladies.
      Reverse, The Treasury paying the Debts of individuals.
14   M. Furius Camillus.
      Reverse, Rome delivered from the Gauls.
15   Manlius causing his Son to be put to death.
      Reverse, Papirius pardoning Fabius.
16   Decius devotes himself for his Country.
      Reverse, the Son follows the Example of the father.

17 The Establishment of the Public Roads.
   Reverse, For the Public Utility.
18 Head of Pyrrhus.
   Reverse, War of Pyrrhus.
19 Military Art.
   Reverse, Majesty of the Senate.
20 Disinterestedness of Fabricius.
   Reverse, Integrity of Fabricius.
21 First Punic War (began 488).
   Reverse, For the Empire of the Sea.
22 Alliance of the Romans with Hiero.
   Reverse, Aid of a faithful Ally.
23 Head of Regulus.
   Reverse, Virtue of Regulus.
24 Taking of Saguntum.
   Reverse, Second Punic War.
25 Head of Hannibal.
   Reverse, Hannibal passing the Alps.
26 Trevia, Trasimene, Cannae, Victories of Hannibal.
   Reverse, Hannibal overcome by Pleasure.
27 Dignity of Soul of Paulus Emilius
   Reverse, Wisdom of the Senate.
28 Revenge sacrificed to the Public good.
   Reverse, Diligence of Claudius Nero.
29 Hannibal at the Gates of Rome.
   Reverse, Spain succoured.
30 Head of Claudius Marcellus.
31 Head of Publius Cornelius Scipio Africanus.
   Continence of Scipio.
32 Scipio passes into Africa.
   Reverse, Interview of Scipio and Hannibal.
33 Scipio, Conqueror of Hannibal.
   Reverse, Rome gives Peace to Carthage.
34 Head of Quintius Flaminius.
   Reverse, Quintius giving the Cup of Liberty to many Persons crowned with
   Flowers, and with this motto, *Liberty restored to Greece.*
35 Asia conquered.
   Reverse, Rome superior to Kings.
36 The noble Defence of Scipio Africanus.
   Reverse, Scipio's Retirement.
37 The Son of Paulus Emilius at Athens.
   Reverse, Paulus Emilius triumphing over Perseus.

PLATE VIII

Emile Lessore, Creamware tablet, 15½″ × 11½″. *The Spring, a sketch for a ceiling.* Signed and dated, 1873

38 Scipio and Lelius, the two Friends.
   Reverse, Third Punic War, began 603.
39 Sedition of the Gracchi.
   Reverse, Jugurtha punished.
40 Head of Marius.
   Reverse, Defeat of the Cimbri.
41 Marius at Carthage.
   Reverse, Horrors of Civil War.
42 Head of Sylla.
   Reverse, Abdication of Sylla.
43 Head of Pompey.
   Reverse, Security of Navigation.
44 Head of Cicero.
   Reverse, Triumph of Eloquence.
45 Pompey, Caesar, and Crassus, united by Ambition.
   Reverse, Conquest of the Gauls.
46 The Death of Mithridates.
   Reverse, Avarice punished.
47 Banishment of Cicero.
   Reverse, Cicero's return from Banishment.
48 Caesar passing the Rubicon.
   Reverse, Flight of the Senate.
49 Caesar and his Fortune.
   Reverse, Intrepidity of Caesar.
50 Battle of Pharsalia.
   Reverse, Humanity of Caesar.
51 Head of Julius Caesar.
   Reverse, Perpetual Dictator.
52 Head of Cato of Utica.
   Reverse, Death of Cato.
53 Head of Marcus Junius Brutus.
   Reverse, the last effort of Liberty.
54 Octavius, Anthony and Lepidus.
   Reverse, Division of the Empire.
55 Anthony and Cleopatra.
   Reverse, Battle of Actium.
56 Augustus.
   Reverse, Reign of Augustus.
57 Head of Agrippa.
   Reverse, Head of Mecenas.
58 Head of Virgil.
   Reverse, Head of Horace.

59 Catullus, Tibullus, and Propertius, represented by three Genii.
Reverse, Head of Ovid and Terence.
60 The Head of Titus Livius.
Reverse, The Head of Sallust.

CLASS V

HEADS OF ILLUSTRIOUS ROMANS, &c.

SECTION I

BEFORE CHRIST

2 inches by 1¾

Romulus.
Numa.
Tullus Hostilius.
Ancus Martius.
Junius Brutus.
M. V. Corvus.
Hannibal.
Scipio Africanus.
T. Quintus Flaminius.
Terence.
Marius.

Sylla.
Pompey the Great, 2 models, a, b.
Cicero.
Cassius.
M. Brutus.
Sallust.
M. Antonius.
Cleopatra.
Varro.
Virgil.
Horace.

AFTER CHRIST

Livy.
Ovid.
Agrippina.
Agrippa.
Perseus.
Seneca.

Julia, daughter of Titus, a, b.
Sabina.
Antinous.
Faustina.
L. J. Rusticus.

3 inches by 2½

Marius.   Cicero.   Augustus.

SECTION III

4 inches by 3.

Junius Brutus.	Cicero
Scipio Africanus.	Pompey.
Marius.	J. Caesar.
Sylla.	Seneca.

CLASS VI

THE TWELVE CAESARS, FOUR SIZES, A, B, C, D
THEIR EMPRESSES, ONE SIZE

The Caesars are from the best Antiques and highly finished.
The Empresses without Frames are 2 inches by 1¾.

BEFORE CHRIST

1 Julius Caesar and Pompea.   2 Augustus and Livia.

AFTER CHRIST

3	Tiberius and Agrippina.		8	Otho and	Poppeia.
4	Caligula	Antonia.	9	Vitellius	Petronia.
5	Claudius	Messalina	10	Vespasian	Domitilla.
6	Nero	Octavia.	11	Titus	Julia, his daughter.
7	Galba	Lepida.	12	Domitian	Domitai.

CLASS VII

SEQUEL OF EMPERORS FROM NERVA TO CONSTANTINE THE GREAT, INCLUSIVE

AFTER CHRIST

13 Nerva.	39 Jul. Philippus.
14 Trajan.	40 J. Philippus Fel.
15 Hadrian.	41 Trajanus Decius.
16 Antoninus Pius.	42 Q. Heren. Decius.
17 L. Verus.	43 Gallus.
18 M. Aur. Antoninus.	44 Volusianus.
19 Commodus.	45 Emilianus.
20 Pertinax.	46 L. Valerianus.
21 Didius Julianus.	47 Gallienus.
22 Pescennius Niger.	48 S. Valerianus.
23 Septimus Severus.	49 Posthumus.
24 Clodius Albinus.	50 Claudius Gothicus.
25 Caracalla, three models.	51 Quintilius.
26 Geta, two ditto.	52 Aurelianus.
27 Macrinus.	53 Tacitus.
28 Diadumenianus.	54 Florianus.
29 Heliogabalus.	55 Probus.
30 Alexander Severus.	56 Carus.
31 Maximinus I.	57 Numerianus.
32 J. V. Maximinus II.	58 Carinus.
33 Gordianus I.	59 Diocletianus.
34 Gordianus II.	60 Maximianus.
35 Pupienus.	61 Constantius.
36 Balbinus.	62 Valerius Maximianus.
37 Gordianus III.	63 Maximinus.
38 Valens Hostilianus.	64 Constantinus.

CLASS VIII

THE HEADS OF THE POPES

These fine Heads are sold at Six-pence a Piece, singly, or at Three-pence a Piece to those who take the Set, which is nearly compleat.

Jesus Christ, A. B. C.   St. Peter, A. B.

1	Linus.	42	Celestine.
2	St. Anacletus.	43	Sixtus III.
3	St. Clement.	44	Leo I.
4	Evaristus.	45	Hilary.
5	Alexander I.	46	Simplicius.
6	Sixtus I.	47	Felix III.
7	Telesphorus.	48	Gelasius.
8	Hyginus.	49	Anastasius II.
9	Pius I.	50	Symmachus.
10	Anicetus.	51	Hormisdas.
11	Soterus.	52	John I.
12	Eleutherus.	53	Felix IV.
13	Victor.	54	Boniface II.
14	Zephirinus.	55	John II.
15	Calixtus.	56	Agapetus.
16	Urban I.	57	Sylverius.
17	Pontianus.	58	Vigilius.
18	Anterus.	59	Pelagius I.
19	Fabianus.	60	John III.
20	Cornelius.	61	Benedict I.
21	Lucius.	62	Pelagius II.
22	Stephen.	63	Gregory.
23	Sixtus II.	64	Sabinianus.
24	Dionysius.	65	Boniface III.
25	Felix.	66	Boniface IV.
26	Eutychianus.	67	Deusdedit.
27	Caius.	68	Boniface V.
28	Marcellinus.	69	Honorius.
29	Marcellus.	70	Severinus.
30	Eusebius.	71	John IV.
31	Melchiades.	72	Theodorus I.
32	Silvester.	73	Martin I.
33	Marcus.	74	Eugenius.
34	Julius.	75	Vitalianus.
35	Liberius.	76	Adeodatus.
*35	Felix II.	77	Domnus I.
36	Damascus.	78	Agathon.
37	Siricius.	79	Leo II.
38	Anastasius.	80	Benedict II.
39	Innocent I.	81	John V.
40	Zosimus.	82	Conan.
41	Boniface I.	83	Sergius I.

84	John VI.	126	Stephen VII.
85	John VII.	127	John XI.
86	Sisinnius.	128	Leo VII.
87	Constantine.	129	Stephen VIII.
88	Gregory II.	130	Martin III, Marinus II.
89	Gregory III.	131	Agapetus II.
90	Zacharias.	132	John XII.
91	Stephen II.	133	Leo VIII.
92	Paul I.	134	Benedict V.
93	Stephen III.	135	John XIII.
94	Constantine.	136	Domnus II.
95	Adrian I.	137	Benedict VI.
96		138	Boniface VII.
97	Leo III.	139	Benedict VII.
98	Stephen IV.	140	John XIV.
99	Pascal I.	141	John XV.
100	Eugenius II.	142	Gregory V.
101	Valentinus I.	143	Silvester II.
102	Gregory IV.	144	John XVI.
103	Sergius II.	145	John XVIII.
104	Leo IV.	146	Sergius IV.
105	Pope Joan.	147	Benedict VIII.
106	Benedict III.	148	John XIX.
107	Nicholas I.	149	Benedict IX.
108	Adrian II.	150	Gregory VI.
109	John VIII.	151	Clement II.
110	Martin II or Marinus I.	152	Damasus II.
111	Adrian III.	153	Leo IX.
112	Stephen VI.	154	Victor II.
113	Formosus.	155	Stephen IX.
114	Boniface VI.	156	Benedict X.
115	Stephen VII.	157	Nicholas II.
116	Theodorus II.	158	Alexander II.
117	John IX.	159	Gregory VII.
118	Benedict IV.	160	Hildebrand.
119	Leo V.	161	Victor III.
120	Christopher.	162	Urgan II.
121	Sergius III.	163	Pascal II.
122	Anastasius III.	164	Gelasius II.
123	Lando I.	165	Calixtus II.
124	John X.	166	Honorius II.
125	Leo VI.	167	Innocent II.

168	Celestine II.	209	Alexander V.
169	Lucius II.	210	John XXIII.
170	Eugenius III.	211	Martin V.
171	Anastasius IV.	212	Eugenius IV.
172	Adrian IV.	213	Nicholas V.
173	Alexander III.	214	Calixtus III.
174	Lucius III.	215	Pius II.
175	Urban III.	216	Paul II.
176	Gregory VIII.	217	Sixtus IV.
177	Clement III.	218	Innocent VIII.
178	Celestine III or Coelestin.	219	Alexander VI.
179	Innocent III.	220	Pius III.
180	Honorius III.	221	Julius II.
181	Gregory IX.	222	Leo X.
182	Celestine IV.	223	Adrian VI.
183	Innocent IV.	224	Clement VII.
184	Alexander IV.	225	Paul III.
185	Urban IV.	226	Julius III.
186	Clement IV.	227	Marcellus II.
187	Gregory X.	228	Paul IV.
188	Innocent V.	229	Pius IV.
189	Adrian V.	230	Pius V.
190	John XX or XXI.	231	Gregory XIII.
191	Nicholas III.	232	Sixtus V.
192	Martin IV.	233	Urban VII.
193	Honorius IV.	234	Gregory XIV.
194	Nicholas IV.	235	Innocent IX.
195	Celestine V.	236	Clement VIII.
196	Boniface VIII.	237	Leo XI.
197	Benedict XI.	238	Paul V.
198	Clement V.	239	Gregory XV.
199	John XXII.	240	Urban VIII.
200	Benedict XII.	241	Innocent X.
201	Clement VI.	242	Alexander VII.
202	Innocent VI.	243	Clement IX.
203	Urban V.	244	Clement X.
204	Gregory XI.	245	Innocent XI.
205	Urban IV.	246	Alexander VIII.
206	Boniface IX.	247	Innocent XII.
207	Innocent VII.	248	Clement XI.
208	Gregory XII.	249	Innocent XIII.

250 Benedict XIII.
251 Clement XII.
252 Benedict XIV.
253 Clement XIII.

254 Clement XIV.
255 Pius VI.
256 Pius VII.

CLASS IX

THE KINGS OF ENGLAND AND FRANCE

These are sold in Sets only.

SECTION I

KINGS OF ENGLAND

1 William the Conqueror.
2 William Rufus.
3 Henry I.
4 Stephen.
5 Henry II.
6 Richard I.
7 John.
8 Henry III.
9 Edward I.
10 Edward II.
11 Edward III.
12 Richard II.
13 Henry IV.
14 Henry V.
15 Henry VI.
16 Edward IV.
17 Edward V.
18 Richard III.

19 Henry VII.
20 Henry VIII.
21 Edward VI.
22 Queen Mary.
23 Queen Elizabeth.
24 James I.
25 Charles I.
26 Oliver Cromwell, Protector.
27 Charles II.
28 James II.
29 William III.
30 Queen Mary II.
31 Queen Anne.
32 George I.
33 George II and Queen Carolina, 2 medals.
34 George III and Queen Charlotte, 2 medals.

SECTION II

ANOTHER SET OF THE KINGS OF ENGLAND IN HIGH RELIEF
INCLUDING THEIR PRESENT MAJESTIES

232

SECTION III

KINGS OF FRANCE

IN SMALL CAMEO

1	Pharamond.	35	Hugues Capet.
2	Clodion.	36	Robert.
3	Merovee.	37	Henri.
4	Childeric.	38	Philip.
5	Clovis.	39	Louis VI.
6	Childebert.	40	Louis VII.
7	Clotaire.	41	Philip II.
8	Clotaire II.	42	Louis VIII.
9	Charebert.	43	Louis IX.
10	Clotaire II.	44	Philip III.
11	Dagobert.	45	Philip IV.
12	Clovis II.	46	Louis X.
13	Clotaire III.	47	Philip V.
14	Childeric II.	48	Charles IV.
15	Theodoric.	49	Philip VI.
16	Clovis III.	50	John II.
17	Childebert III.	51	Charles V.
18	Dagobert III.	52	Charles VI.
19	Chilperic II.	53	Charles VII.
20	Theodoric II.	54	Louis XI.
21	Childeric III.	55	Charles VIII.
22	Pepin.	56	Louis XII.
23	Charlemagne.	57	Francois I.
24	Louis.	58	Henri II.
25	Charles the Bald.	59	Francois II.
26	Louis II.	60	Charles IX.
27	Louis III and Carloman.	61	Henri III.
28	Charles II.	62	Henri IV.
29	Eudes.	63	Louis XIII.
30	Charles III.	64	Henri IV.
31	Robert.	65	Louis XIV.
32	Louis IV.	66	Louis XV.
33	Lothaire.	67	Louis XVI and Marie-Antoinette.
34	Louis V.		

CLASS X

HEADS OF ILLUSTRIOUS MODERNS, FROM CHAUCER TO THE PRESENT TIME

These Heads are made either in the *black Basaltes*, or *blue* and *white Jasper*; they are of various Sizes and different Prices, from One Shilling a piece to a Guinea, with and without Frames of the same Composition; but most of them in one Colour and without Frames are sold at One Shilling each.

* * *

SECTION I

ENGLISH POETS

2 Inches by 1¾ without Frames

1	Geoffrey Chaucer.	13	Oldham.
2	John Gower.	14	Otway.
3	Sir Philip Sidney.	15	Waller.
4	Spencer.	16	Earl of Surrey.
5	Beaumont.	17	Dryden.
6	Shakespeare, several Models.	18	Addison.
7	Fletcher.	19	Congreve.
8	Johnson.	20	Prior.
9	Cowley.	21	Lansdowne.
10	Milton.	22	Pope.
11	Butler.	23	Swift.
12	Rochester.	24	Garrick, several Models.

SECTION II

PAINTERS

1	Leonardo da Vinci.	6	Corregio.
2	Michael Angelo.	7	Anibale Carracci.
3	Titiano.	8	La Seueur.
4	Rafaelle da Urbino.	9	Francisco Albani.
5	Gulio Romano.	10	Carlo Maratti.

SECTION III

PHILOSOPHERS, PHYSICIANS, &c.

1 Francis Verulam, Lord Bacon.
2 Galileo.
3 Gassendi.
4 Descartes.
5 Sir Isaac Newton, A.B.C.
6 Sir William Hamilton.
7 Linnaeus.
8 Mr. Edwards.
9 Mr. Blake, late of Canton in China.
10 Locke.
11 Rousseau.
12 Dalembert.
13 Diderot.
14 Montagne.
15 Dr. Haller.
16 Condamine.
17 Burlemaqui.

18 Dr. Friend.
19 Fontanelle.
20 De Moivre.
21 Van Sweiten.
22 Dr. Benjamin Franklin, A.B.C.
23 Nicholas Keder.
24 Mr. Banks.
25 Dr. Solander.
26 Mr. Pennant.
27 Dr. Foster.
28 Ray.
29 Dr. Mead.
30 Dr. Woodward.
31 Dr. Hans Sloane.
32 Dr. Pemberton.
33 Captain Cooke.
34 Doctor Priestley.

SECTION IV

DIVINES, ARTISTS, ANTIQUARIES, POETS, &c.

1 Melancthon ⎱ a pair.
2 Erasmus ⎰
3 Inigo Jones ⎱ Ditto.
4 Sir Christopher Wren ⎰
5 Mons. Boileau ⎱ Ditto.
6 Mad. Dacier ⎰
7 Milton, Model C ⎱ Ditto.
8 Oliver Cromwell ⎰
9 St. Evermond ⎱ Ditto.
10 Voltaire ⎰
11 Montesqueiu ⎱ Ditto.
12 Milton, Model B. ⎰
13 Conyers Middleton — with Cicero, Class V.
14 Charles Rinald Berch.
15 Dr. Stukely.

16 Magliabechi.
17 Mr. S. More.
18 Cardinal Mazarine.
19 Endymion Porter.
20 Lord Camden.
21 Lord Chesterfield.
22
23 Duke of Montague.
24 Preville.
25 Sully.
26 De Sartine.
27 Crebillon.
28 Moliere.
29
30 Agnes Soreau.
31 Henry IV.

235

32	Andrew Fountaine.	50	Madame Montespan.
33	Gonzalez.	51	Fenelon.
34	Mad. Clairon.	52	Boileau.
35	Mad. Du Boccage.	53	Fontaine.
36	Marchioness Pompadour.	54	Madame Des Houlieres
37	Marchioness Du Chatelet.	55	Pascal.
38	Peter Corneille.	56	Ninon de Lenclos.
39	Marchioness de Savigne.	57	Racine.
40	Marquis Maffei.	58	Blaise Pascal
41	Marmontel.	59	Peter Gassandi
42	Coysevox.	60	Fenelon, Abp. of Cambray
43	Countess Grignan.	61	Turenne
44	Madame Dacier.	62	Des Cartes
45	Laura.	63	Boileau
46	Countess de la Sage.	64	Grotius
47	Countess du Barre.	65	Grotius, 4 inches by 3.
48	Madame de Scuderie.	66	Barnevelt, ditto.
49	Madame d'Estree MS. of Monceaux.		

Small medals (58–64)

CLASS XI

PRINCES AND STATESMEN

1	Amurat I.	16	Louis XV.
2	Antonius, King of Navarre.	17	Louis XVI, A.B.
3	Henry IV of Grance, A.B.C.	18	Queen of France.
4	Sully.	19	Sir Robert Walpole, A.B.
5	Queen Elizabeth.	20	John Duke of Marlborough.
6	Christiana, Queen of Sweden.	21	John Sobieski, King of Poland.
7	Charles I and Mary.	22	Augustus II, King of Ditto.
8	Charles II.	23	Marshal Count Saxe.
9	Charles XII of Sweden, A.B.	24	Cardinal Noialles.
10	Colbert.	25	Louis Bourbon, Prince of Condé.
11	Cardinal Fleury.	26	James Stuart.
12	Peter the Great of Russia, 17 inches by 14.	27	William III.
13	Peter Alexis, Son of Peter the Great.	28	George I.
		29	George II.
14	Cardinal Mazarin.	30	Late Prince of Wales.
15	Louis XIV, A.B.C.	31	Princess Dowager of Wales.
		32	George III, A.B.C.

33	Queen Charlotte, A.B.C.	39	Earl of Shannon.
34	Duke of Bedford, Regent of France.	40	King of Prussia.
35	Algernon Sydney.	41	Prince Henry of Prussia.
36	Lord Chatham, A.B.C.	42	King of Sweden.
37	Washington.	43	Admiral Keppel.
38	Duke of Courland.		

CLASS XII

BUSTS, SMALL STATUES, BOYS, ANIMALS, &c.

The black Composition having the Appearance of *antique Bronze*, and so nearly agreeing in Properties with the Basaltes of the Aegyptians, no Substance can be better than this for Busts, Sphinxes, small Statues, &c. and it seems to us to be of great Consequence to preserve as many fine Works of Antiquity and of the present Age as we can, in this composition; for when all Pictures are faded or rotten, when Bronzes are rusted away, and all the excellent Works in Marble dissolved, then these Copies, like the antique Etruscan Vases, will probably remain, and transmit the Works of Genius, and the Portraits of illustrious Men, to the most distant Times.

Those who duly consider the Influence of the *fine Arts* upon the *human Mind*, will not think it a small Benefit to the World to diffuse their Productions as widely, and to preserve them as long as possible; for it is evident, multiplying the Copies of fine Works in durable Materials, must have the same Effect upon the *Arts* as the Invention of Printing has upon the *Sciences*; by these Means the principal Productions of both Kinds will be for ever preserved; and most effectually prevent the Return of Ignorant and barbarous Ages.

Upon these Considerations, we have, at a very considerable expence, extended the Subjects of this Class, and endeavoured to give them all the Perfection in our Power; and we hope the Articles in the following List will be found to merit the Notice of those who have been pleased to honour us with their generous Patronage.

SECTION I

BUSTS

About 25 inches high

| M. Aurelius Antoninus. | Junius Brutus. |
| Lord Chatham. | Marcus Brutus. |

Zeno.
Plato.
Epicurus.

Antinous.
Augustus.
Antoninus Pius.
Inigo Jones.

Cato.
Faustina.
Rousseau.
Cicero.
Socrates.

Lord Bacon.
Johnson.
Raleigh.

Young Germanicus.
Ditto Marcus Aurelius.

Homer.
Democritus.
Hippocrates.
Galen.
Aristotle.
Cicero.
Vestal.
Zingara.
Chaucer.
Beaumont.
Fletcher.
Shakespeare.
Milton.
Congreve.
Prior.
Swift.

Pindar.
Homer.

About 22 inches high
Palladio.
Demosthenes.
Minerva.

About 20 inches high
Dr. Swift.
Horace.
Grotius.
Seneca.

About 18 inches high
Newton.
Venus De Medicis.
Boyle.

About 16½ inches high
Agrippina.

About 15 inches high
Pope.
Plato.
Sappho.
Julia.
Seneca.
Virgil.
Addison.
Dryden.
Horace.
Johnson.
Spencer.
Madona.
Madona.
Locke.
Newton.

About 11½ inches high
Cicero.

About 10 inches high

Locke.   George II.
Newton.   Voltaire.

About 8 inches high.

Socrates.   M. Anthony.
Aristotle.   Cleopatra.

About 7 inches high

Newton.   Prior.
Locke.   Congreve.

About 4½ inches high

Homer.   Ariadne.
Bacchus.   Voltaire.

About 4 inches high

Montesquieu.   Aristophanes.
Rousseau.   Voltaire.
Pindar.

SECTION II

STATUES, ANIMALS, &c.

1 Neptune, 2 feet.
2 Triton, 2 ditto.
3 Polyphemus, 19 inches by 16.
4 Morpheus, a reclining Figure, 25 Inches long.
5 Ceres, a Girl sitting.
6 Infant Hercules, with the Serpent, 20 inches high by 21 broad.
7 Ganymede, from the Florentine Museum, 12 inches.
8 Bacchus, from Sansovino, 11 inches
9 Ditto, from Michael Angelo, 11 inches.
10 Egyptian Lions, from the Capitol, 8½ inches long by 5 high.
11 Five Boys, from Fiamingo, 5 inches long.
12 Egyptian Sphynxes, a Pair, 6 inches long.
13 Grecian Sphynxes, ditto, 12 inches long.
14 Ditto, 5 inches.
15 Egyptian ditto, with the Lotus, to hold Candles, 6 inches long.
16 Sitting Sphynxes, with Nossles, to hold Candles, 10¾ inches.

17	Griffins, with ditto, 13 inches by 7.	23	Apollo, a Statue, 11 inches.
18	Elephants, 16½ inches long by 14½ high.	24	Venus Medicis, 10½ inches.
19	A Pair of Tritons, from Michael Angelo, 11 inches high.	25	Mercury, 11 inches.
20	Bacchus, a Statue, 10¾ inches high.	26	Mr. De Voltaire, 12 inches.
21	Fawn, ditto.	27	Venus rising from the Sea, upon a Pedestal, richly ornamented with Figures, representing the Seasons, 6½ inches.
22	Two Pug Dogs.		

CLASS XIII

VARIOUS KINDS OF LAMPS AND CANDELABRIA, USEFUL AND ORNAMENTAL

These Lamps are both of the variegated Pebble and Black Composition. They bear the Flame perfectly well, and are fit for Chambers, Halls, Stair-Cases, &c.

The Tripod Lamps with several Lights are highly enriched, and will be suitable Ornaments for the finest Apartments. The Prices of the Lamps from Two Shillings a Piece to Five Guineas.

The Candelabria are after antique Models, and of various Kinds and Prices, from Two Shillings and Six-pence a Piece to Sixteen Shillings.

CLASS XIV

TEA-POTS, COFFEE-POTS, SUGAR-DISHES, CREAM-EWERS, WITH CABINET CUPS AND SAUCERS, OF VARIOUS KINDS, IN THE ETRUSCAN STYLE

The Tea-pots are of several Compositions, both plain and painted with Etruscan and Greek Ornaments, from Six-pence to about Twelve Shillings a Piece. The other Pieces are made to match them, and to compose Dejeunés and Tea Equipages at proportionate Prices.

CLASS XV

FLOWER-POTS OF VARIOUS KINDS

Of these there is a great Variety of Patterns, both for Roots and dressing with Flowers; the first from Six-pence to Six or Seven Shillings a Piece; the latter, or Vase Flower-pots, from One Shilling a Piece to Eighteen Shillings, or more, according to the Composition and finishing.

CLASS XVI

ORNAMENTAL VASES

OF ANTIQUE FORMS, IN A COMPOSITION OF TERRA COTTA, RESEMBLING AGATE, JASPER, PORPHYRY, AND OTHER VARIEGATED STONES, OF THE VITRESCENT OR CRYSTALINE KIND

These Vases are adapted for the Ornament of Chimney-Pieces, Cabinets, Bookcases, &c. — They are from six Inches to eighteen or twenty Inches high. The Prices from Seven Shillings and Six-pence to Two or Three Guineas a Piece, according to their Size and Manner of finishing, with Handles, Draperies, Festoons, Medallions, &c. They are generally sold in *Pairs*, or Sets of *three, five*, or *seven Pieces*. The Sets of five Pieces sell from about Two Guineas to Five or Six Guineas a Set.

CLASS XVII

ANTIQUE VASES, OF BLACK PORCELAIN, OR ARTIFICIAL BASALTES,

HIGHLY FINISHED, WITH BAS-RELIEF ORNAMENTS

Of this Species of Vases we have a great Variety of Forms; the Sizes from three or four Inches high to more than two Feet. The Prices from Seven Shillings and Six-pence a piece to Three or Four Guineas, excluding the very large ones, and those pieces which consist of many Parts, and are very highly finished. The Sets of *five Pieces*, for Chimney-pieces, sell from about *Two* Guineas to Six or Eight Guineas a Set. From all the Specimens we have seen, and the Observations of others, we have reason to

241

conclude, that there are not any Vases of Porcelain, Marble, or Bronze, either ancient or modern, so *highly finished*, and *sharp in their Ornaments*, as these Black Vases; and on this Account, together with the Precision of their Out-lines, and Simplicity of their antique Forms, they have had the Honour of being highly and frequently recommended by many of the Connoisseurs in Europe; and of being placed amongst the finest Productions of the Age, in the Palaces and Cabinets of several Princes.

CLASS XVIII

PAINTED ETRUSCAN VASES, PATERAS, &c.

The *Vases* of this Class, as well as the *Paintings*, are copied from the Antique with the utmost Exactness; as they are to be found in *Dempster*, *Gorius*, Count *Caylus*, *Passerius*, but more especially in the most choice and comprehensive Collection of *Sir William Hamilton*; which, to the Honour of the Collector, and of this Nation, and for the Advantage of our Artist, is now placed in the British Museum.

The Art of painting Vases in the Manner of the Etruscans has been lost for Ages; and was supposed, by the ingenious Author of the Dissertation on Sir *William Hamilton's* Museum, to have been lost in Pliny's Time. The Proprietors of this Manufactory have been so happy as to re-discover and revive this long lost Art, so as to have given Satisfaction to the most critical Judges; by *inventing* a Set of *Encaustic Colours*, essentially different from *common Enamel Colours*, both in their *Nature* and *Effects*, as will be more minutely explained in another Article; and by the Discovery of a Composition proper to receive them.

And as it is evident the finer Sort of *Etruscan Vases*, found in *Magna Graecia*, are truly Greek Workmanship, and ornamented chiefly with Grecian Subjects, drawn from the purest Fountain of the Arts; it is probable many of the Figures and Groupes upon them, preserve to us Sketches or Copies of the most celebrated Grecian Paintings; so that few Monuments of Antiquity better deserve the Attention of the Antiquary, of the Connoisseur, and the Artist, than the *painted* Etruscan Vases.

There are already Specimens of these three Kinds of Vases, or some of them, in the Apartments or Cabinets of

Our Illustrious Sovereigns.
The Empress of Russia.
The King of Poland.
The King of Prussia.
The King of Sweden.
The King of Denmark.
The King of Portugal.

The Grand Duke of Tuscany.
The Elector of Saxony.
The Prince of Mecklenburg Shwerin.
The Marquis of Pombal.
The Landgrave of Hesse Cassel.
Madame the Landgravess of Hesse Cassel.
The Duke Regent of Brunswick.

The Prince Czartoriskie.
The Baron de Coccy.
The Duke Regent of Saxe-Gotha.
The Duke of Arunburg.
The Duke of Wurtemberg.
The Prince of Anhalt Bernbarg.
The Prince of Anhalt Coethen.
The Prince of Anhalt Dessau.
The Landgrave of Hesse-Darmstadt.

The Landgrave of Hesse Hombourg.
The Margrave of Anspach.
The Margrave of Brandenburg Schwedt.
The Margrave of Bade Durlach.
The Prince of Saxe Cobourg.
The Duke of Saxe Weymar.
The Duke of Holstein Beck.
The Duke of Courland.
The reigning Prince of Salm Salm.

CLASS XIX

VASES, EWERS, &c. ORNAMENTED WITH ENCAUSTIC PAINTINGS

When the Proprietors of this Manufactory carefully inspected some original Etruscan Vases (shewn them by his *Grace the Duke of Northumberland*) with *a View of imitating them*, it was the general Sense of all the Connoisseurs and Antiquaries who spoke on this Subject, that the *Art was lost*; and afterwards, when Sir *William Hamilton's* Book was published, and with a truly liberal Spirit presented to them by Sir *Watkin Williams Wynn*, this Sentiment was not only confirmed but such a Description given of the Difficulties of the Art itself, as was sufficient to damp all Hopes of Success, in attempting to revive it: but the Proprietors had happily made a considerable Progress in their Discovery before they read this discouraging Account; being set to work by some Proof Sheets of *Sir William Hamilton's* Book, put into the Hands of Mr. *Wedgwood* by Lord *Cathcart*; and having carefully inspected the above mentioned, and some other Collections of Etruscan Vases, that were then in *England*, as well as perused with Attention all that the late illustrious Count *Caylus* had written upon Etruscan Antiquities.

When the Manufacturers had carefully examined the original Etruscan Vases, they were convinced that the Colours of the Figures could not be successfully imitated with *Enamel*; and that their Success in attempting to revive this lost Art would chiefly depend upon the Discovery of a new Kind of *enamel Colours*, to be made upon *other Principles*, and have *Effects* essentially different from those that were then in Use, and are of the Nature of Glass: the Etruscan Colours being without *any glassy Lustre*.

In Consequence of this Observation, and by a great Variety of Experiments, this Discovery has been made, and a Set of *encaustic* Colours *invented*, not only sufficient completely to imitate the Paintings upon the Etruscan Vases; but to *do much more*; to give to the Beauty of Design, the Advantages of Light and Shade in various Colours; and to render Paintings durable without the Defect of a varnished or glassy Surface.

An Object earnestly desired by Persons of critical Taste in all Ages, and in modern Times, without Success.

The ingenious Experiments of Count *Caylus* to make *encaustic Pictures* had the same Object as ours, in Point of Taste; but his Use of *Wax* in Compliance with the Letter of *Pliny*, had he succeeded ever so well in the Execution, must have rendered his Pictures very liable to be injured by any considerable Degree of Heat to which they might have been exposed; and the Manner of applying the Colours was liable to many Difficulties and Inconveniencies. It is evident this Kind of Painting, in *coloured Wax*, has little or no Resemblance to ours but in Name.

Our Encaustic *Colours* can be applied with great Ease and Certainty; they change very little in the Fire; are not liable to run out of Drawing; are perfectly durable, and not glassy; they have *all the Advantages of Enamel*, without its *essential Defects*.

We thought it necessary to give this short History and Description of an Art which is *new to the public*, and which we hope will appear, by the suitable Application of it to merit their Attention: but a better Idea of it than can be conveyed in Words, may be formed by those who please to examine the Specimens of this Art that belong to this and the following Class.

The Figures upon these Vases are taken chiefly from Gems, antique Paintings, and Bas-reliefs; and are executed with great Care by the best Hands we can employ. We have spared no Attention to render them fit Ornaments for the noblest Apartments: and considering the great Expence and Risque attending such delicate Subjects, the Prices are *much lower* than those of any other Ornaments in Europe, that can with Propriety admit of Comparison with them.

The Vases painted in this Way are from 6 or 8 inches to 20 inches high; and of various Prices, from one Guinea a piece to ten or twelve Guineas.

CLASS XX

TABLETS

AND PICTURES FOR CABINETS AND INLAYING, UPON PLATES OF THE ARTIFICIAL BASALTES, AND UPON A NEW KIND OF ENAMELLED PLATE.

These Paintings may be applied, and have already been applied, to great Advantage in Chimney Pieces and Cabinets: and when the *Effects* are observed, and the *durable Nature* of the Work considered, we hope the Application of them will be greatly extended.

Since the first Edition of this Catalogue, we have had the good Fortune to execute many large Tablets, in a great Variety of Colours, with Success; and as the Colours do not run out of Drawing, are smooth, durable, and without any vitreous Glare, this is acknowledged, by Persons of the most refined Taste, to be a higher and more perfect Species of Painting than was known to the World before the Date of this Invention; and therefore it is hardly necessary to add, that *no Art is capable of producing richer or more valuable Decorations*.

These Tablets may be made from the Bracelet Size to Pieces of Eighteen or Twenty Inches Diameter, and from One Guinea to Fifteen or Twenty Guineas a piece: but the Price depends upon so many Circumstances, attending the Execution, that it is not easy to give any satisfactory Idea of it in Writing. It varies according to the Size of the Plates, the Number of Figures, the Merit of the Hands employed, and the Degrees of *finishing*. All persons are sensible that Works of great *Risque* and *Expence* cannot be executed without being sold for proportionate Prices; and in this Instance the Artist can truly say, they have the *smallest Profit* upon their *highest Works*.

CLASS XXI

INK STANDS, PAINT-CHESTS, EYE-CUPS AND MORTARS

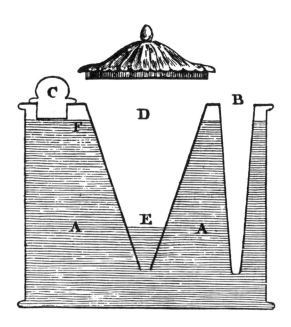

The Proprietors of this Manufactory have made a considerable Variety of Ink Vessels and Ink-stands; but the best and most convenient that has every been brought into Use, they apprehend, is one represented in the above Engraving, and which being new, will require some Explanation.

EXPLANATION OF THE PLATE

A. A. The Ink Cistern filled with Ink up to F.

B. Pen Tubes which are closed at the Bottom, and therefore do not admit any Air into the Cistern.

C. An Opening that communicates with the Cistern; and an Air-tight Plug.

D. A Cone through which the Vessel is filled; first taking out the Plug C, and then pouring in the Ink till the Cone is full; after which the Plug must be returned to its Place, and the Ink poured out of the Cone, or taken out with a Spunge, down to E. The Ink will then remain in the Cistern at F. and the Vessel act as a Fountain; the Pen taking up the Ink through the Cone D. at E.

PROPERTIES OF THE INK-STAND

This Ink-stand, on Account of the gradual Opening of the Cone, is not liable, like the common ones, to soil the Pen and Fingers.

The narrow End of the Cone prevents the Pen from striking aginst the Bottom.

The Surface of the Ink is exposed to the Air only at one small Point E, whereby it is prevented from evaporating, and from growing thick and spoiling, which is the Case in all the common Ink-stands, where a large Surface is unavoidably exposed to the Air.

And it is a further Recommendation of these *Ink-stands*, that they are made of a very fine and compact Black Jasper, or Porcelaine, that neither corrodes with the Ink nor absorbs it; and that they admit of being finished, and that many of them are constantly finished with the utmost Accuracy, so as to be fit to accompany the finest Works of Art in any Part of Europe.

These Ink Vessels are sold separately, as they are represented in the above Plate, or with Sand Boxes, Wafer Boxes, &c. forming various Kinds of useful and ornamental Ecritoire; the Prices from Six-pence, gradually rising, according to the Sizes, Forms, and Workmanship, to about Eight Shillings each.

The *Paint-Chests* contain Sets of large and small Vessels, and neat Palats, for the Use of those who paint in Water colours, and sell at Five Shillings to Ten Shillings and Sixpence each Chest.

The *Eye-Cups* are of the Composition imitated variegated Pebbles, and are very convenient for bathing the Eyes; price One Shilling each.

The Mortars will be of great Use of *Chymists, Experimental Philosophers and Apothe-*

caries, as well as for culinary Purposes; not being liable, like Metals or Marble, to be corroded by Acids or any other chemical Menstruum.

*   *   *

CONCLUSION

The Proprietors of this Manufactory, hope it will appear to all those who may have been pleased to attend to its Progress, that ever since its Establishment it has been continually *improving*, both in the Variety and the Perfection of its Productions.

A Competition for *Cheapness*, and not for *Excellence* of *Workmanship*, is the most frequent and certain Cause of the rapid Decay and entire Destruction of Arts and Manufactures.

The Desire of selling much in a little Time, without respect to the Taste or Quality of the Goods, leads Manufacturers and Merchants to ruin the Reputation of the Articles which they manufacture and deal in: and whilst those who buy, for the Sake of a falacious Saving, prefer Mediocrity to Excellence, it will be impossible for Manufacturers either to improve or keep up the Quality of their Works.

This Observation is equally applicable to Manufactures, and to the Productions of the fine Arts; but the Degradation is more fatal to the latter than the former: for though an ordinary Piece of Goods, for common Use, is always dearer than the best of the Kind, yet an ordinary and tasteless Piece of Ornament is not only *dear* at any Price, but absolutely useless and ridiculous.

All Works of Art must bear a Price in Proportion to the Skill, the Taste, the Time, the Expence, and the Risque attending the Invention and Execution of them. Those Pieces that for these Reasons bear the highest Price, and which those who are not accustomed to consider the real difficulty and Expence of making *fine Things*, are apt to call [illegible] when justly eliminated, the *cheapest* Articles that can be purchased, and such as are generally attended with much less Profit to the Artist than those that every body calls *cheap*.

There is another Mistake that Gentlemen who are not acquainted with the Particular Difficulties of an Art, are apt to fall into. They frequently observe that a handsome Thing may be made as cheap as an ugly one. A moment's Reflection would rectify this Opinion.

The most successful Artists know they can turn out ten ugly and defective Things for one that is beautiful and perfect in its Kind. Even suppose an Artist has the true Idea of the Kind of Beauty at which he aims, how many lame and unsuccessful Efforts does he make in his Design, and every Part of it, before he can please himself? And suppose one Piece is well composed and tolerably finished; as in Vases and encaustic Paintings, for instance, where every succeeding Vase, and every Picture, is made, not in a Mould or by a Stamp, but separately, by the Hand, with the same Attention and

247

Diligence as the first, how difficult must it be to preserve the Beauty of the first Model!

It is so difficult, that without the constant Attention of the Master's Eye, such Variations are frequently made in the Form and Taste of the Work, even while the Model is before the Workman, as totally change and degrade the Character of the Piece.

Beautiful Forms and *Compositions* are not to be made by Chance; and they never were made, nor can be made in any kind at a small Expence: but the Proprietors of this Manufactory have the Satisfaction of knowing, by a careful Comparison, that the Prices of many of their Ornaments are *much lower*, and of all of them as *low* as those of any other Ornamental Works in *Europe*, and of equal Quality and Risque, notwithstanding the high Price of Labour in *England*; and they are determined, rather to give up the making of any Article, than to degrade it. They do not manufacture for those who estimate Works of Ornament by their *Magnitude*, and who would buy Pictures at *so much a Foot*: they have been happy in the Encouragement and Support of many illustrious Persons, who judge of the Works of Art by better Principles; and so long as they have the Honour of being thus patronized, they will endeavour to support and improve the Quality and Taste of their Manufactures.

FINIS

SIXTH EDITION OF WEDGWOOD'S CATALOGUE 1787

Bas-relief subjects added in the sixth and last edition of the Catalogue (1787) are as follows: (the attributions are Miss Meteyard's)

		Measurements	*Artist*
235	The frightened horse, from Mr. Stubbs' celebrated picture, and modelled by himself	11¼ by 17½	Stubbs
236	The fall of Phaeton, modelled by the same	12 ,, 21½	,,
237	A Roman procession	9½ ,, 21	
238	An offering to Peace; from a design of Lady Templeton. Dec. 1777	6½ ,, 11½	Templeton
239	The same; smaller size		,,
240	Friendship consoling Affliction; from the same	7 ,, 8¾	
	The same, different sizes, to	3 ,, 4	
241	Group of three boys, from designs of Lady Diana Beauclerk	5½ ,, 4½	Beauclerk
242	Group of two boys, from the same	5½ ,, 4½	,,
	The same, different sizes, to	3½ ,, 2¾	
243	Four boys, single, from the same	4½ ,, 3¾	,,
	The same, different sizes, to	3 ,, 2¼	
244	Bacchanalian tablet of the six preceding articles, under arbours, with panthers' skins in festoons, &c.	16 ,, 5½	
245	Venus in her car drawn by swans, with attendant Cupids, &c. from Le Brun	4¼ ,, 9	Le Brun
246	Cupid watering the swans, &c. from the same	4¼ ,, 9	,,
247	Domestic employment; from a design by Miss Crewe	3½ ,, 4¼	Miss Crewe
	The same, different sizes, to	1½ ,, 2	
248	Domestic employment	4½ ,, 5¾	Templeton
249	Family School, and companion; from the same	4½ ,, 5¾	,,
	The same, different sizes, to	2 ,, 3¼	
250	Study, and its companion; from the same	3 ,, 3¾	Templeton
	The same, different sizes	1¾ ,, 2¼	,,

		Measurements		Artists
251	Maria, from the same	3 ,, 3¾		Templeton
	Bourbonnois shepherd; its companion	3 ,, 3¾		
	The same, different sizes, to	1¾ ,, 2¼		,,
252	Genii, from Lady Templeton; measured diagonally	3 ,, 7		,,
	The same, different sizes, to	1¾ ,, 3¾		,,
253	Companion to the foregoing	1¾ ,, 3¾		,,
254	Infant Academy, from a picture by Sir Joshua Reynolds, different sizes from	5 ,, 6¼		
	Music, its companion, sizes from	2½ to 3¼		
255	Blindman's Buff; a group of boys. 1782	5½ by 13		Flaxman
	The same, smaller sizes, to	3 ,, 9		,,
256	Commercial Treaty with France. Jan. 16, 1787	11 ,, 9		,,
257	The same subject differently expressed, March 26, 1787			,,
258	Coriolanus, with his wife and mother persuading him to return to Rome	6 ,, 9¾		,,
259	Sacrifice to Hymen	10		Webber
	Sacrifice to Concordia, its companion	10		,,
260	Offering to Love	4½ ,, 5¾		
	Conjugal fidelity, its companion	4½ ,, 5¾		
	The same	4½		
261	The river Thames, different sizes from	2¾ to 3½		
	Isis, its companion ,, ,, ,,	2 ,, 3		
262	Jupiter, eagle, and Ganymedes	3½ by 2¾		
263	Triumph of Cybele	3¼ ,, 6		
264	Hymen	5 ,, 6¾		
265	Apotheosis of Homer	7½ ,, 15½		Flaxman
266	,, ,, Virgil	7½ ,, 15½		,,
267	Cupid sharpening his arrows	5		
268	Cupid stringing his bow	5		
269	The Graces erecting the statue of Cupid	10¾ ,, 9		Webber
270	The young sempstress, and companion;	4 ,, 2½		Crewe
	The same, different sizes, to	2¼ ,, 1¼		
271	Sportive Love	4 ,, 3¼		Templeton
	The same, different sizes, to	2¾ ,, 2¼		
272	Charlotte at the tomb of Werther, from the same	5 ,, 4		,,
	The same, different sizes, to	2¾ ,, 2¼		
273	Contemplation, and its companion, from the same	4 ,, 3¼		,,

		Measurements		Artists
274	Diana visiting Endymion; from the celebrated bas-relief in the Capitol at Rome	$8\frac{1}{2}$,,	$27\frac{1}{2}$	Flaxman
	The same, smaller sizes, to	—	—	,,
275	Hercules in the garden of the Hesperides from a beautiful Etruscan vase in the collection of Sir William Hamilton, now in the British Museum. Aug. 1787	$5\frac{1}{2}$	17	,,

UNCATALOGUED BAS-RELIEFS

1	The education of Bacchus	
2	A triumph of Mars	Webber
3	A boy leaning on his quiver, with doves	,,
4	Hebe; its companion	
5	Cupid; a model	
6	Proserpine; a bas-relief	Devaere
7	Discovery of Achilles	,,
8	Orestes and Pylades prisoners on the shores of Scythica	,,
9	Judgment of Paris; remodelled	,,
10	Achilles and the daughters of Lycomedes	,,
11	The Muses, with figures reclining	Pacetti
12	Priam kneeling before Achilles, begging the body of his son Hector	,,
13	The fable of Prometheus	,,
14	The triform goddess Luna, Diana, and Hecate	,,
15	The simulacrum of Hygiea	,,
16	A Faun, with three Spartan Bacchantes	,,
17	Endymion sleeping on the rock Latmos	,,
18	Marcus Aurelius making his son Commodus Caesar	,,
19	Apotheosis of Faustina	,,
20	The nine Muses	,,
21	Thetis in childbed with Achilles	,,
22	Palmyra; an oval tablet modelled for Daguerre, 1788	Unknown
23	Death of Cato; a tablet in basaltes, 1774	,,
24	Death of Peter the Great; a tablet in basaltes	,,
25	The triumph of Achilles over Hector	Pacetti
26	Apollo and the muse Erato	Angelini
27	Pluto carrying off Proserpine, preceded by Hercules	,,
28	Victory and Mercury	,,
29	The fable of Meleager	,,
30	Apotheosis of a young prince	,,

		Artist
31	Two Fauns	Angelini
32	Two Bacchantes	,,
33	Silenus	,,
34	Pleasures of the Elysian fields	,,
35	An offering to Ceres	Flaxman
36	Peace, Labour, and Plenty; an oval bas-relief	Webber
37	Dance of Cupids; after Raffaelle	
38	Bacchanalian dance; 19½ in. by 8 in.	
39	Agamemnon, Achilles, and Briseis, 10¾ in. by 8½ in.	Flaxman
40	The Nereides	Dalmazzoni
41	The Vitruvian Scroll, 1785	Westmacott
42	Masque of Alexander, 1786	Webber
43	Triumph of Mars	Webber
44	Nymphs decorating the statue of Priapus	Webber
45	Roman Procession	Dalmazzoni
46	Procession to Isis; from an Egyptian vase. Encaustic painted and archaic.	
47	Proserpine; a bas-relief, 1788	Devaere
48	Teletes and Socrates; a masque	Hackwood
49	Lion and horse, 15½ in. by 10 in. (Prior to 1783)	

'MODERN' PORTRAIT SUBJECTS ADDITIONAL TO THOSE LISTED IN THE 1779 CATALOGUE

King of Spain.
Pius VI.
Prince Lambertini.
Gustavus, King of Sweden.
Empress of Russia.
Prince of Russia.
Duke of Courland.
Joseph II of Germany (two models).

Frederick the Great of Prussia.
Frederick William III of Prussia.
Prince of Lignes.
Prince of Brunswick.
William I of the Netherlands.
Queen of ditto.
Wilhelm, first Prince of Orange.
Louise de Coligny, Princess of ditto.

Wilhelm-Frederic, hereditary Prince of
    ditto.
Princess Fred. Wilhelmina Louisa of
    ditto.
Henry IV.
Charles I.
Oliver Cromwell.
Prince of Wales, afterwards George IV.
Duke of York.
Prince William Henry.
Prince Ernest Augustus.
Prince Augustus Frederic.
Prince Adolphus Frederic.

STATESMEN AND COMMANDERS

Duke de Bouillon.
Temminck, Lord Burgomaster.
Cornelius de Witt.
John de Witt.
Michael Ruyter.
Peter Hein.
Rombout Hogerboots.
Egbert Kortenaar.
Baron Reden.
Lord Hood.
Lord Amherst.
General Elliot.
General Monkton.
Governor Franklin.
Duke of Northumberland.
Marquis of Rockingham.
Earl of Shannon.
Earl Cowper.
Earl of Sandwich.
Lord Hillsborough.
Lord Mansfield.
Lord North.
Lord Hawkesbury.
Bishop of St. Asaph.
Sir John Phillips.
Sir William Dolben.

Right Hon. William Pitt.
Right Hon. H. Dundas.
Hon. Warren Hastings.
Mr. Montague.

PHILOSOPHERS AND NATURALISTS

Bergman.
Kaempfer.
Sir Ashton Lever.

PHYSICIANS

Boerhaave.
Dr. Fothergill.
Dr. James Fordyce.
Dr. Buchan.

PAINTERS

Sir Joshua Reynolds.
Mr. West.
Mr. Byres.
Sir William Chambers.
Mr. Wyatt.

ANTIQUARY

Mr. Stuart.

DIVINES AND MORAL WRITERS

Dr. Johnson (two models).
Jonas Hanway.

LADIES

Duchess of Devonshire.
Lady Banks.
Lady Charlotte Finch.
Mrs. Montague.
Mrs. Barbauld.
Mrs. Kennicott.
Mrs. Siddons.

SECOND EDITION OF CATALOGUE

Leopold, Emperor of Germany.
George, Prince of Denmark.
William, Duke of Gloucester.
Charles XI of Sweden.
Charles Emanuel, Duke of Savoy.
William Maximilian, Duke of Brunswick
Lady Orford.
Mrs. Hay.
Count Gyllingburg.
William, Duke of Cumberland.
The Queen of Denmark.
Martin Luther.
Averanius Benedict.
Martin Ffoulkes.
Vander Mulan.
William Bridgeman.
Dr. Baker.

Sir John Barnard.
Gay.
Addison, inscribed Bickerstaff.
Thomson.
Louis Francis Le Fevre.
Louis de Boucherat.
Christia Francia, Duchess of Suabia, and
    Queen of Cyprus.
Cardinal Rochefoucauld.
Tellier, Chancellor of France.
Archbishop Laud.
Biragus René.
Lord Molesworth.
John Gordon.
Louis Gervaise.
William de Lamoignon.
Lord Molesworth.

FOURTH EDITION

Nicholas Keder.

Coysevox.

SELECT BIBLIOGRAPHY

History of the Staffordshire Potteries, Simeon Shaw. 1829.

Life of Josiah Wedgwood, Eliza Meteyard. London, 1865.

The Wedgwoods' being a life of Josiah Wedgwood, Llewellyn Jewitt. London, 1865.

Handbook of Wedgwood Ware, Eliza Meteyard. London, 1875.

Old Wedgwood, F. Rathbone. London, 1893.

Josiah Wedgwood, Samuel Smiles. London, 1894.

Josiah Wedgwood, Master Potter, A. H. Church. London, 1903.

Wedgwood's letters to Bentley, edited by K. E. Farrer. London, 1903.

The Imperial Russian Dinner Service, Dr. George C. Williamson. London, 1909.

The Makers of Black Basaltes, M. H. Grant. London, 1910.

Josiah Wedgwood and his Pottery, William Burton. London, 1922.

Wedgwood Ware, Harry Barnard. 1924.

Wedgwood Ware, W. B. Honey. London, 1948.

The Portland Vase and the Wedgwood Copies, Wolf Mankowitz. London, 1952.

Old Wedgwood, Wedgwood Club of America.